SEXY
christians
WORKBOOK

For Individuals, Couples, *and* Small Groups

DR. TED ROBERTS &
DIANE ROBERTS

BakerBooks

a division of Baker Publishing Group
Grand Rapids, Michigan

Published by Baker Books
a division of Baker Publishing Group
P.O. Box 6287, Grand Rapids, MI 49516-6287
www.bakerbooks.com

Printed in the United States of America

ISBN 978-0-8010-7241-3 (pbk.)

Published in association with Yates & Yates, www.yates2.com.

Contents

Introduction

This Is Going to Be Fun!

TED

I remember the first time we did a Sexy Christians Seminar. A local television station showed up and interviewed several of the participating couples. One comment stands out in my mind: Smiling from ear to ear, the wife told the reporter, "We're going home to work on this stuff. This is going to be fun!"

I pray you have this same attitude of joyful expectation as you walk through the *Sexy Christians Workbook* together. During our seminars we tell participants that if they do the exercises we provide, they will save at least $2,000 in counseling costs. We've led thousands of couples through these assignments over the last few years and witnessed amazing results. I promise you: the Holy Spirit desires to do the same miraculous work in your marriage. We only ask that you invest in this workbook with passion and vulnerability toward one another and God.

Some of you may be thinking, *We have a great marriage. We don't need counseling. And I'm not sure we need a work-*

book. Congratulations! What Diane and I have learned through the years is that the Sexy Christians principles and exercises make great marriages incredible. And who doesn't want an incredible marriage?

Others may have picked up this workbook as a last-ditch attempt to save a marriage. But I challenge you: *don't give up or lose hope*. Marilyn vos Savant, listed in the *Guinness Book of World Records* as the person with the world's highest IQ, made a fascinating observation: "Being defeated is often only a temporary condition. Giving up is what makes it permanent."[1]

You may be thinking, *Some folks are just lucky. They have a talent for having a great marriage. But my spouse and I are a different story. No marriage talent here. And we don't have the kind of talent to study stuff like this either. Where's the hope?* However, recent research reveals that folks who believe talent is fixed and innate view challenges, mistakes, or tough times as threats to their ego instead of opportunities to improve. This causes them to lose confidence and motivation when the work gets hard. As a result, they end up in a condition called *learned helplessness*.[2]

Once the honeymoon is over and you get down to the hard work of marriage, the enemy can easily set you up to believe your relationship is hopeless. He leads you to think having to work hard on your marriage shows your inability. Instead, having to work hard simply shows you're one real person married to another real person. And God can use as small a number as one to change *everything*!

Unfortunately, many couples today are having serious problems in their sex lives. As we mention in the *Sexy Christians* book, the National Health and Social Life Survey ("The Sex Survey") was a 1992 landmark study that surveyed 1,749 women and 1,410 men between the ages of eighteen and fifty-nine. The research revealed that adults of all ages experience sexual problems, and 43 percent of women and 31 percent of men reported having a sexual problem *in the prior year*.[3] Given the tendency of Christians to connect shame and embarrassment with sexual problems, these startling results are probably much lower than the actual numbers.

And if the level of divorce and the number of couples living together outside of marriage are indicators, things haven't improved in the years since the study. In fact, back in 1992 approximately half the men reported extramarital affairs, and studies since then indicate women are reaching the same level of infidelity.[4]

Put all this together and you realize that at some point in their relationship nearly every couple has difficulties with sex and intimacy. One of the saddest commentaries on the depth of marital and sexual struggles in our day are the ubiquitous commercials and emails selling "male enhancement products." I imagine your computer's junk mail file, like mine, overflows with the silly things. I didn't think much about it until I spoke about human sexuality at a Christian college. At one of the sessions, I addressed the young men exclusively and asked if they had any questions. One young man shot up his hand to ask which of these "male enhancement products" was best. I couldn't help but chuckle as I pointed out a woman's vagina only has nerve endings in the first two and a half inches. Besides, only 6 percent of women are ever concerned about the size of their partner's genitals.[5]

We all have times in our marriage when things aren't exactly magical. Let me declare to you as strongly as I can: *that's normal*! Problems or struggles are simply God's way of calling our attention to the fact that we each bring our own set of issues into marriage. Whenever an issue presents itself, a couple has a wonderful opportunity to pull together and talk openly and, in the process, learn the magic of deep intimacy.

The Challenge

On the surface the human sexual response cycle is a straightforward reflex response, similar to the patellar reflex that occurs when someone taps your knee. When your genitals receive enough stimulation, they'll respond. Raise this response to a certain level and orgasm will occur.

At this point things can get very interesting. We humans give meaning to nearly everything that touches us. The meanings we bring to our sexual feelings (past and present) directly affect how our bodies react to sexual stimuli. The feelings we have about the sensations we experience directly determine the level of our sexual satisfaction. This shows the magic and mystery of being human. Past relationships can easily intrude into the present and affect our sexual responsiveness.

Our most significant relationship, however, is the one we have with God. From this relationship arises the one we have with ourselves. In fact, how you feel about what you are feeling can be a primary determining factor in your overall sense of sexual fulfillment. If you believe your sexuality offends God, you will feel horrible about being you. This can become a deeply agonizing cycle of frustration, guilt, and shame.

We see a much different picture, however, in people who are *comfortable* with their sexuality as a precious gift from God, *vulnerable* with their mate, and *devoted* to spiritual growth. Here we find an indescribable experience of intimacy that reaches down to the essence of their being and unites them with the person they love.

The experience of intimacy is an active, changing one. Three dynamic factors determine our response to sexual stimulation:

1. The type of sensory stimulation we are receiving
2. Our body's ability to react or respond to that stimulation
3. Our emotional perception of the stimulation (as noted above, how we feel about being aroused can either free us or chain us)

How can something that seems so natural become so difficult? Let's think about all three factors. The type of stimulation we desire and respond to, unique to each of us, is our *arousal template*. This term refers to the mental patterns of our experiences and conditioning that define what we consider sexually arousing. Also, our body's ability to respond to sexual stimulation changes through the years. The

Massachusetts Male Aging Study revealed that 52 percent of males ages forty to seventy have difficulty achieving or maintaining an erection.[6] And as mentioned earlier, the National Health Survey reported that adults of all ages experience sexual problems.[7] Add to that our emotional perceptions of what is stimulating (which can also be deeply affected by our experiences) and you come to only one conclusion: *biblical intimacy can be a real challenge*.

Yes, you will have to work to achieve the kind of intimacy God intends for your marriage. We call this the *Sexy Christians Workbook* because it's going to take *work*. But let me assure you, true biblical intimacy is worth every moment you spend and every ounce of energy you expend to achieve it. Why? Because God designed you for intimacy with him and with your spouse. As Jesus expressed so beautifully,

> My prayer is not for them alone. I pray also for those who will believe in me through their message, that all of them may be one, Father, just as you are in me and I am in you. May they also be in us so that the world may believe that you have sent me. I have given them the glory that you gave me, that they may be one as we are one.
>
> John 17:20–22

True biblical intimacy carries a purpose, power, and passion like nothing else because of the transforming touch of Christ on our lives, individually and as a couple. We can only touch one another in true intimacy if we willingly move toward what we call the three *R*s of biblical intimacy:

Revisit the wounds of our past through the gift of marriage.

Refine our hearts through the strength of God's grace.

Respond to our calling together in Christ.

Through the pages of this workbook, we'll explore numerous opportunities to encounter all these and more. Get ready for work, play, and marital intimacy as you've never before experienced it. This is going to be fun!

T.O.U.C.H. Points

How to Use This Workbook

TED AND DIANE

Before we go any further, let's explain a little about how we've organized our workbook so you can maximize its impact in your life and marriage. First, this study adds depth and practicality to our book *Sexy Christians: The Purpose, Power, and Passion of Biblical Intimacy*. You will understand this workbook best if you've already read that material or if you study the two books alongside each other. You will also want to keep a Bible handy so you can refer to it for the Bible study points mentioned in each chapter.

Sexy Christians defines *biblical intimacy* as "developing the ability to be uncomfortably close and vulnerable with another imperfect human." We also explain that the phrase *Sexy Christians* isn't an oxymoron but a mark of God's original design. True intimacy as God intended it is a huge but rewarding challenge.

We have organized the workbook contents around the acronym T.O.U.C.H.

Trust

Openness

Understanding

Critical Conversations

Honesty

Each chapter covers one of these key areas in detail and serves to expand and underscore the great truths in *Sexy Christians*. We've packed each chapter so full of helpful information and exercises that we want you to allow plenty of time to study each one carefully. You (or even better, both of you) should plan two or more study sessions per chapter to read the material, process it, and share your answers. You might consider a weekly date night when you go over your Personal Touch exercises and then do another activity you both enjoy. (Who knows? If the study goes well enough, you may not need to leave the house!)

Because of the interactive, often personal nature of the assignments, it is best for each person to have his or her own copy of the workbook. To assist couples with book costs, groups or churches may wish to pool funds or provide scholarships. Check out the "Tell Me More" section at the end of this book for information on group discounts.

Although we often refer to sharing answers with your spouse, we understand that each situation is different. Please don't let your spouse's unwillingness or inability to study this material with you keep you from pursuing it yourself. God will honor your pursuit of a more intimate marriage whether your mate studies the Sexy Christians material or not.

Format

Because the content of each chapter varies, the components also vary somewhat, but we have incorporated several consistent elements. Each chapter uses the T.O.U.C.H. format to explore each chapter topic through various methods.

IN TOUCH

A true story of someone who applied the Sexy Christians principles and saw God at work. We have changed names to preserve anonymity.

TOUCH UP

A short Bible study that supports the chapter teaching. It is sometimes split into several parts.

TOUCH DOWN

Teachings and explanations that apply Sexy Christians principles to the specific T.O.U.C.H. focus of the chapter. This may also be split and occur two or more times within a chapter.

PERSONAL TOUCH

Thought-provoking questions, exercises, and points for self-examination and dialogue with your mate that help you personalize the teaching and adapt it to your own marriage. You will find these Personal Touch exercises scattered throughout the Touch Up and Touch Down sections of the material.

If you're in a group, make it a priority to read the appropriate pages and complete the Personal Touch exercises *before* the session in which you cover the material (see appendices 4 and 5 for study plans). The rules for sharing Personal Touch are the same as the rules for Home Play in *Sexy Christians*:

1. Avoid "you" statements. Instead, talk about your own actions, thoughts, and feelings.
2. Listen. Don't give advice or attempt to psychoanalyze your spouse.
3. If tempers flare, disengage and pray.

FINISHING TOUCH

Concluding challenges and other elements to help summarize the chapter teaching and ensure its practical use in your life as a Sexy Christian.

Additional Features

We have also incorporated two special features into each lesson to help make the *Sexy Christians Workbook* as helpful as possible. Look for them in the margins of this workbook.

QUICK QUOTES

Brief, helpful excerpts from our book *Sexy Christians*.

LEADER LINES

Leaders' hints, group questions, and other suggestions for those leading a Bible study, Sunday school class, or other small group through this material.

Small Group Study

You can study the *Sexy Christians Workbook* alone or (if possible) with your mate, but you will receive the most benefit from the material if you follow up your personal study with a small group. This can be a group of friends or neighbors, a Bible study or Sunday school group, accountability partners, or almost any other small group interested in studying the material together.

Are you a small group leader? Turn to appendix 1 to read our specific tips for taking a group through this material. Appendices 2 and 3 contain material for the introductory and final sessions. Appendices 4 and 5 contain suggested schedules to customize the material for your small group study.

1

Trust

Core of Growing Intimacy

Ted

"Lord, please help John in his job, and Bob needs your healing touch." I open my eyes for a moment. Joe and I are kneeling beside our bed. He is praying aloud, lost in his concern for our friends. The prayers are not profound, yet they fill me with a sense of safety. We are together, Joe is talking honestly with our God, and I can trust God to be talking to him.

Trust—easily lost, so hard to regain. How well I know this. Joe started an affair with a girl in our church when I was pregnant with our third daughter. He left to live with her for six months and then returned home—physically, but not emotionally. Three difficult years later, in response to Joe's cry for help, God moved us halfway around the world for a new start as a family. How we struggled through those next

The Sexy Christians challenge:

revisit your past wounds.

17

years. "Listen to my heart," Joe would say. "I'm for you, not against you." I found that so hard to believe.

Gradually, though, I began to trust my husband again. Proverbs 14:1 became one of my favorite verses: "The wise woman builds her house, but with her own hands the foolish one tears hers down." How often I tore down the house we were trying to build. Slowly I learned that Joe needed my encouragement. It takes a lot of courage for a man to move beyond the shame of his choices and the effects they have on his family. As Joe's wife, I had a key role in his success.

Now, as we pray together, I sensed again his desire for this new life to work. In the past it was easy for me to criticize those prayers, to wish they were more personal, wordier, more like mine. But as I expressed my appreciation, Joe's prayers changed. We changed. We got into ministry together, encouraging others with things we had learned the hard way. We learned to communicate, to listen beyond the words we said to the heart behind them. We began to play together and laugh together. I learned to trust his heart.

Today we celebrate nearly forty years since the day we first said our vows. Our appreciation of each other is huge. Our celebration that we are together to enjoy our daughters and grandchildren is constant. And our compassion for those who struggle is immense. Truly, God does bring beauty from ashes and restores trust when it has been destroyed.—Janice

TOUCH DOWN

I didn't grow up as a regular church attender, and one of the things I couldn't understand when I first started attending church was the way everyone talked about how much they loved it when Jesus answered their prayers. I always thought that was a no-brainer, but:

What do you do when he doesn't respond?
What do you do when your life is in crisis mode and all you get is silence?

Lead in prayer as you begin. Ask members to reread or recall the In Touch testimony printed here and give one-word responses (*wow*, *hope*, etc.). Record these on your whiteboard or butcher paper. Point out that because of your varied backgrounds and experiences you will often have different responses to the material, but God's Holy Spirit will personalize the truth. Because of our hope in Christ, no situation or marriage is hopeless.

*What do you do when you pray with all your might about
your marriage and things only get worse?*

*What do you do when your spouse seems oblivious to
your needs?*

*What do you do when old patterns of response within you
cripple your ability to love the one you married?*

It doesn't take long to realize being in love—with a spouse
or with the Lord—doesn't mean problems never come your
way. They will come because, amazingly enough, problems
are a key part of the intimacy process.

Earlier we pointed out that the acrostic T.O.U.C.H. forms
the framework for this workbook. In chapter 1 we start with
the letter *T*. When we seek to deepen our sense of intimacy
in marriage, we begin by deepening our *Trust* in God.

"Why do you say that?" you might ask. The answer is
simple: *you are one imperfect person married to another
imperfect person*. If you've been married for more than five
minutes, I'm sure you've noticed your spouse's imperfec-
tions. The truth is, you are deeply flawed as well. If this
weren't true, you wouldn't need a Savior. In fact, if you
intend to achieve true biblical intimacy, you must (individually and as a couple) face the difficult challenge of revisiting
your past wounds. This process can feel like a crucifixion,
so you need to know and believe in a God who can resur-
rect you both.

Frequently our wounds from the past become the force
that stands between us and true intimacy with God and our
mate. If we don't revisit these wounds, they can become
grossly enlarged rearview mirrors that block our view of
God's blessings. Whenever the past defines the future, we're
headed for relational conflicts. In fact, if we stay focused on
life's past wounds, we can end up driving off the road or
into one another.

"Every living, breathing individual carries wounds from the past. Often these wounds have been stuffed deep inside our souls like a snake hiding in a flowerbed. When we don't deal with them, the resultant anger seeps through us like poison and affects every relationship and experience we encounter."
—*Sexy Christians*

PERSONAL TOUCH

Use no more than three sentences to describe a time in your life when God showed himself trustworthy.

_____

_____

_____

_____

_____

_____

_____

Next, briefly describe a time when you felt disappointed with God.

_____

_____

_____

On a scale of 1–5 (1 lack of trust, 5 complete trust), circle your current level of trust with God.

1	2	3	4	5
Lack of trust				Complete trust

Take time to discuss your answers with your spouse and explain the reasons behind the level of trust you circled.

Flip this Personal Touch around by asking participants to share, first, times when they felt disappointed with God and second, times when they saw his trustworthiness. Model good listening skills by giving each speaker your full attention and addressing each one by name.

TOUCH UP

We all feel frustrated sometimes. Even the best of us can find ourselves dealing with anger against God.

Let's look at John 11. In this passage Mary, who is famous for sitting attentively at Jesus's feet, wrestles with anger. It's one of those times when nothing seems to be working. Her brother, Lazarus, is seriously ill and getting worse by the minute. She sends word to Jesus, asking him to come and help, but he won't respond. She feels the same way you and I do when we don't see an immediate answer to our prayers or when we do things right and they seem to turn out wrong.

Most of us want Jesus to panic right along with us. We expect him to show up on the scene and fling open the door of the ambulance right before it leaves for the hospital. Better yet, he could arrive before we call the rescue squad. Our Lord seems to miss every opportunity for an early appearance, yet he is never late.

Do you know the story? Jesus never makes it to the house or the hospital. He doesn't even make it to the funeral or graveside service. Jesus finally shows up after Lazarus has been dead for *four days*! Mary, the one who loved so deeply, is deeply wounded. You can hear it in her words: "Master, if only you had been here, my brother would not have died" (John 11:32 Message).

Have you ever gone through an experience when you couldn't figure out what Jesus was doing? If you have been walking with the Lord more than a day or two you have. Sometimes we hurt and Jesus doesn't seem to care. We're in deep need and he doesn't rush to our side. Our head knows he has a reason, but our heart screams so loudly we can barely think straight. And if we find it difficult when the Lord doesn't seem to care about our needs, we find it nearly impossible not to overreact when our spouse shows the same attitude.

 PERSONAL TOUCH

Draw a picture of a time you saw evidence that your mate cared about something you cared about too.

"The couple must learn to trust not only God but other people as well. Since almost all of our deep wounds are created within the context of human relationships, our healing comes in relationships as well. We can't change or find restoration in a vacuum."—*Sexy Christians*

Before the meeting, enlist a group member to share about a time of personal need when Jesus's response came later than anticipated. Read John 11:1–18, 31–32 aloud. Then ask the group member to share as planned. How did God use the delay for good? As time permits, allow others to share similar situations and experiences.

Draw a picture of a time when you felt your spouse showed a lack of concern for something you felt was important. Share both pictures with your mate if possible.

TOUCH DOWN

What does Mary's story have to do with our stories? Chronic frustrations with our spouse and with God can keep us from breaking through to deep intimacy in either relationship. The key: chronic frustration often has its source in the wounds of our past, not the pressure of the present.

During the first years of our marriage, Diane used to frustrate me with her constant stream of questions about an upcoming decision or event. Amidst these incessant inquiries, I'd remain calm for a while. Eventually, though, I'd become so irritated I'd fire back, "Don't you think I know what I'm doing? Don't you think I have a brain?"

As soon as those fiery responses left my mouth, I knew they were wrong. They hurt my wife, but I couldn't seem to stop myself. I justified my behavior with inner comments: *She should respect me more. How can I be her spiritual leader if she is constantly second-guessing every decision I make?* In my heart I knew there was a deeper problem, but I couldn't identify it.

One day when Diane's questions came my way again, I stopped and examined my emotions. I felt like a kid, criticized and smothered all at once. That's when the lights went on.

I loved my mom deeply, but when I became a teenager and started pulling away, her alcoholism triggered some deep insecurities. In Mom's attempt to hold on, she overwhelmed me with attention. As a single mom, her fears of abandonment unleashed a torrent of questions and criticism.

Diane, however, is a classic problem solver who loves to figure out situations and resolve difficult issues. She intended her questions as part of a helpful, joint process, and my angry responses mystified and wounded her. Of course all of this was a perfect set-up from heaven to heal me and bring Christ's resurrection power to bear on my life. But Satan had the opposite intention: provoke us into deeply wounding each other and use the conflict to tear our marriage apart.

PERSONAL TOUCH

Over- or under-reacting to situations often indicates a wound from the past. The following questions can help you discover the source of the wound and understand why the past so powerfully impacts the present.

Recall a time when you over-reacted (exhibited an extreme response like yelling or running away) or under-reacted (withdrew or pushed down your anger) during a disagreement or difficult situation. Describe it in a few sentences.

_____

_____

_____

As you look back, how could you have responded in a more balanced fashion? Again, use a few sentences to respond.

_____

_____

_____

_____

Sometimes fears underlie our anger and can trigger an over- or under-reaction. Examine the fears or issues listed below.

"Good grief occurs when we recognize the patterns of woundedness or immaturity in our lives and cry out to God for help. I call it *good* grief because it releases healing to those areas of our lives that have caused us so much pain. Good grief is more than good. It's *great* grief because it heals."
—*Sexy Christians*

Read the preceding quote aloud. If possible, share an example of a time in your life when you experienced good grief. Ask participants to recall one area of woundedness in their life. Lead them in a prayer of repentance, asking the Holy Spirit to bring healing and wholeness. This marks the end of part A for the twelve-week plan. Review next week's Home Play assignments as you close the session.

Circle any you believe may serve as triggers or sources for the anger you experienced in the present.

Feelings of abandonment	Loss of control
Rejection	Feeling controlled
Humiliation	Lack of support
Criticism	Lack of time together
Feeling like a failure	Lack of intimacy
Money or financial issues	Confrontation
Feeling inadequate	Trust issues
Lack of communication	Parenting issues
Relational issues with extended family	Work pressures
Other: _____	

TOUCH DOWN

The turning point came when I cried out to God about my anger toward Diane and received nothing but silence in response. *Christ loved me enough not to show up.* He was touching my life with tough love—the kind of love that is willing to offend in order to heal. His love delayed him.

You see, if he had come on the scene immediately, I would never have realized the hidden wounds I carried. Christ could have soothed my hurting heart, I could have apologized to my wife, but nothing would have changed inside. Real intimacy would never have had a chance to take root and grow. Trust would have been destroyed because eventually I would have reacted out of frustration and anger once again.

PERSONAL TOUCH

Complete the chart that follows.

Column 1: List the frustrations you presently experience in your marriage as honestly as you can. The object is not to create a weapon but to develop a tool to improve your marital intimacy.

Column 2: Identify your level of frustration. Notice the three examples provided.

Column 3: Attempt to identify the hope beneath this frustration.

Column 4: Give a numerical rating to the hope you listed in column 3. The results of this final column could take your intimacy to the next level.

Column 5: Ask the Holy Spirit to reveal any connection between a high level of hope you have in the present (from column 3) and a hurt from your past.

Frustrations: I am troubled by or when my spouse. . . .	Level of frustration (1 low, 10 high)	Related hope for my marriage	Level of hope (1 low, 10 high)	Past hurt that lies beneath that hope
Example 1: *spends too much money*	9	*to be debt-free*	3	*As I was growing up, our family lived from paycheck to paycheck. I am fearful of doing the same.*
Example 2: *doesn't meet my sexual needs*	8	*to be compatible in our sexual desires*	2	*Love was withheld in my family of origin; my needs were not met.*
Example 3: *won't let me perform at his club*	9	*to star with Ricky in a movie*	8	*I grew up poor and no one noticed me.*

Groups following the twelve-week plan should begin part B here. Before today's session, prepare a large copy of the chart on page 25. Point out the example using Lucy Ricardo and ask members to help compose responses for another fictional character. If the situation allows, and with your spouse's permission, share a personal frustration and its connection to a past hurt and present hope. Emphasize your woundedness more than your frustration.

TOUCH UP

When Mary finally comes to Jesus with her deep frustrations over his lack of response, Jesus asks only one thing: "Where have you laid him?" (John 11:34). He is asking her to show him the place where she stopped hoping and believing he could do the impossible. The miracle can't occur until Mary leads Jesus to the spot where her faith had stretched to its breaking point.

In the tension of hopes and frustrations in marriage, we can begin to give up on our dreams. But we won't find the solution by fixing or changing our partner. Yes, marriage is a refining process, and Christ will help both partners improve. But if we never address our own core wounds (hurts from the past), our partner can never change enough. And the underlying frustrations have little to do with our partner anyway.

In the premarital process, if I discover the wife- or husband-to-be has an anger problem, I ask the couple to delay the marriage until they address this issue. Otherwise they will find themselves involved in irresolvable conflicts because the angry partner reacts in the present out of the context of wounds from the past. This is usually an unconscious process that arises from the limbic system or, as Scripture terms it, the "heart" (fundamental thoughts and emotions).[1]

Did you find the Personal Touch uncomfortable? Mary did. This process can be uncomfortable for everyone. Remember the *Sexy Christians* definition of biblical intimacy: "developing the ability to be *uncomfortably close* and vulnerable with another imperfect human." Sometimes the process is so uncomfortable it stinks. When they arrive at the gravesite, Jesus tells them to remove the stone that seals the tomb. Mary's sister, Martha, makes a cogent observation: "Lord, by now the smell will be terrible because he has been dead for four days" (John 11:39 NLT).

PERSONAL TOUCH

I'm so thankful we follow a Savior who loves us too much to let the stinky stuff stop him. He doesn't hesitate to get involved in the muck and mire of our lives, and he won't give up on us when we've given up on ourselves. He walks with us to the place where we stopped believing.

On the lines below, write one or more things you can agree to work on as a couple this week.

> For example: "My spouse and I will look at our finances together and agree on a budget."

_____

_____

_____

_____

TOUCH DOWN

We all have places where we stopped believing God can do the miraculous. We've all given up hope at some point because life has hit us so hard. Those who have been abused or mistreated carry deep pain within. Often we don't want others—even God—to see our pain.

For years I lived that way, in pure survival mode. After all, Mary couldn't have left Lazarus lying on the living room couch, could she? She had to get on with life. We've all done it. But Jesus's love for us is so rich that he tells us to roll the stone away. He urges us to tear down the defenses we've built to wall off our pain. He constantly asks us to roll away doubt and fear, to take the limitations we have placed on God, and to throw them away. He wants to make us Sexy Christians. Will we let him?

PERSONAL TOUCH

Until you roll away the stone by recognizing your past wounds and how they affect you, they will continue to hijack your brain. You have learned to react rather than respond, and anger or other emotions are your natural or limbic response to past fears.

Use a few words to identify a recent example of an event or person that elicited an angry response from you.

_____

_____

_____

List any additional emotions you felt at the time.

_____

_____

_____

Revisit the list of fears you circled on page 24. Can you identify one or more as a possible factor that made your anger more volatile in the situations you listed here? Explain them in a sentence or two and then discuss it with your mate.

_____

_____

_____

God often asks us to do things that don't make sense to the rest of the world. Briefly describe a time when God asked you to do something illogical (for example: tithing when your financial resources were low; quitting a job without another one in sight).

_____

_____

_____

What were the results of that step of faith?

_____

_____

_____

___	Noah (Gen. 6:13–16)	a. be born again
___	Abraham (Gen. 22:1–2)	b. drop your nets and follow Jesus
___	Hosea (Hosea 1:2)	c. marry a prostitute
___	Nicodemus (John 3:3)	d. build a gigantic boat in the desert
___	Peter and Andrew (Matt. 4:18–19)	e. sacrifice your long-awaited son

Prepare the chart on the left in advance (use your whiteboard or butcher paper). As a group, match each person with his outlandish assignment from God. (For answers, see endnote 2 for this chapter).

TOUCH UP

Sometimes Jesus's deepest healing words don't make a bit of sense. God's love toward us contains what I call *divine wildness*. His love is scandalous, unconditional, and above all, sovereign. He knows exactly where we need to grow in grace when we don't have a clue.

God fills his love letters with examples of his crazy love. Immediately after Joshua leads Israel across the Jordan River and into the Promised Land, God commands him to gather all the troops together. I'm sure Joshua must be thinking, *This is going to be great. God's going to destroy those enemy armies at last, and we can all watch the victory.*

Talk about a rude awakening! Instead of inviting the Israelites to a victory celebration, the Lord asks them to drop their drawers for a circumcision party (Josh. 5:2–3). For the next few days, they walk around like a bunch of bowlegged cowboys while surrounded by hostile armies. Apparently God is more concerned about their inner relationship with him than the external problems they face. *That doesn't make a bit of sense.*

Next, the circumstances grow more ridiculous. Joshua realizes a military citadel, the walled city of Jericho, stands in the way of his people walking fully into the Promised Land. What is God thinking? Then he tells the Israelites to walk around Jericho's outside walls. For six days they have to remain silent, but on the seventh day they are to strike up the band for a shouting tour around the city. Then God will knock the walls flat. *That doesn't make a bit of sense.*

I could point to many incidents in Scripture that don't make a bit of sense. You've already examined several. But some of the craziest words God shares with us refer to how awesome we are in his eyes.

PERSONAL TOUCH

Read the following Scriptures and write them out in your own words. Then personalize them by adding your name where the Bible uses a more general term like *beloved* or *world*. If you are sharing this exercise with your spouse, trade books and read each other's versions aloud. Do your best to look into your partner's eyes as you speak of God's deep and abiding love.

Example: "I have loved Ted with an everlasting love; I have drawn him with loving-kindness" (Jer. 31:3).

Psalm 32:10

_____

_____

John 3:16

_____

_____

John 15:9

_____

_____

"God cares for you deeply. If you follow his pathway for relationships, he will graciously touch your life. He will faithfully pour out his richest blessings upon you and your mate."
—*Sexy Christians*

Through the ages, God has sought to tell his children of his love. Ask several group members to read their personalized versions of Scripture aloud. Remind them that true biblical intimacy starts with an intimate relationship with God. Pray aloud for group members' spiritual growth, or worship together by listening to a selection from a praise CD. Be sensitive to individual needs.

TOUCH DOWN

The pattern is clear: *the crazier the words from God, the deeper the healing.* No, Christ does not ask us to disconnect our brains. Instead he asks us to confront the mental patterns and roadblocks of the past that prevent us from experiencing intimacy and fulfillment. Only God the Holy Spirit can lovingly walk beside us to the gravesite of our deepest wounds and challenge us to roll the stone away. Only he can help us remove the mental and emotional coping systems we've developed. If we desire to achieve true biblical intimacy, we must move beyond survival mode into a genuine relationship of trust.

I was sitting in a clinical training seminar after three days of studying and sharing together. This time, though, the emotional stakes were sky-high. The instructor challenged us to investigate areas where we might carry past hurts that affected us in the present. That's when the Holy Spirit whispered, *It's time to share it all*.

I had not purposely hidden anything. Still, when I tried to communicate, I met frustration. I hadn't found anyone with whom I could share the emotional wounds of my combat experiences. Either I received the glazed professional counselor look ("Yes, I understand; tell me more. How are you feeling?") or the dilated eyes and shocked expression of the nonprofessional. Neither addressed my true feelings. Why would I want to move the stone away? So each time I decided to pour another layer of concrete over it instead.

This time, however, the Holy Spirit was asking me to roll the stone completely away. *But Lord, I don't want to look like a basket case!* Fortunately, I recognized the destructive nature of that thought. Attempting to protect appearances destroys any possibility for growth in intimacy with God and others.

But I faced a second problem. My therapy partner was an elegant Ph.D. candidate from Peru. What could she possibly know about my trauma? Yet the Holy Spirit repeated the crazy words, *Share everything*.

I began slowly, watching my partner's reaction. Soon her eyes filled with tears as she tenderly spoke the exact words I needed to hear. It turned out she had taken part in a political demonstration in Peru. She had joined with other women to protest the violent abuse by the ruthless military dictator in power at the time. She knew this could mean her immediate death or imprisonment.

The night before the march, my partner asked her young daughter if she thought her mom should participate. She was a single parent, and even a simple arrest could spell disaster. The next morning her daughter said, "Mom, you need to march for us both."

I listened as she described the march. The protesters turned the corner and headed toward the presidential palace. A line of troops awaited, rifles aimed directly at them. I can't tell her story as eloquently as she did, but miraculously, she survived.

Now I was weeping while we shared our pain. As I rolled the stone away, I came to see how deeply God loves me. His sovereign grace brought his healing touch through a marvelous new friend. And as Jesus promised Martha in John 11, *if you roll the stone away, you will see the glory of God.* That day, I saw his glory at close range.

PERSONAL TOUCH

Is there a stone you need to roll away? Is there a wound beneath the irritation in your relationship? Is it time for you to experience a new level of God's glory in your marriage?

Complete the chart on the next page, allowing yourself time to listen to the Holy Spirit's guidance. Your responses can bring your marriage to new levels of glorious intimacy.

Share your answers with your spouse if possible, but be careful not to demand help. Instead, let this exercise become a vulnerable expression of where you are in your healing journey with Christ.

TOUCH UP

One thing can keep us from removing the stone no matter how much we may want to do so. Mary and Martha struggle with it in John 11 as they wrestle with their anger. Unresolved anger leads to *unforgiveness*—the ultimate killer of our intimacy with Jesus and others. Jesus sums up the destructiveness of unforgiveness and the power of trusting him in a parable found only in Luke 17:4–6.

> "If he sins against you seven times in a day, and seven times comes back to you and says, 'I repent,' forgive him." The apostles said to the Lord, "Increase our faith!" He replied, "If you have faith as small as a mustard seed, you can say

"After several decades of counseling others, I've realized something: I have never had to counsel a couple who prays together every night."—*Sexy Christians*

Take time to discuss how this study has helped group members grow in the *T* area of trust. Reflect back to Janice's In Touch testimony and remind members of the way mutual prayer helped this couple's intimacy grow. Encourage couples to move toward the habit of praying together daily.

What lies behind my stone (past wound or other area of pain)?	What must I do to move the stone? (How can I reveal it?)	How can others help me?
Example 1: *Sexual Abuse*	*Admit it is still a problem.*	*Seek a counselor or group to help process the wound from the past.*
Example 2: *Betrayal*	*Honestly confront and process this event.*	*Meet with a group, friend, or counselor to help process the pain.*

to this mulberry tree, 'Be uprooted and planted in the sea,' and it will obey you."

I have often wondered about this little parable. For example, why does Jesus say, "this mulberry tree"? It turns out only Luke uses this term,[3] obviously in reference to a specific type of tree. Ancient Jewish writers have noted its extensive root structure that make it difficult to uproot.

Since the context of the parable is the disciples' struggle with hurt and unforgiveness, the implications seem obvious. Unforgiveness causes problems because, like the mulberry tree, it quickly develops a root structure deep within our soul.

Because of its rapid growth, the mulberry tree was frequently used to build caskets. It usually grew in arid conditions and wasps pollinated it.[4] Your unforgiveness can sting you or bury you. Isn't it time to let go?

PERSONAL TOUCH

This section includes questions designed to help you roll the stone away by confronting wounds of the past. These won't become a part of group discussion but will help you understand and apply Sexy Christians principles.

Below list people who have hurt you in the past and then give a brief description of what happened and how you felt at the time.

Person's name	Description of what happened	Emotions felt
Example: *Authority figure*	*1. Made promises but never followed through, which impacted my wages. (Betrayal)*	*1. Anger, hurt, unforgiveness* *2. Fearful of authority figures*

Now list some common themes you see in your list—such as betrayal, feeling devalued, abuse, gender-related injustice, or a need to please in order to obtain love.

1. _____
2. _____
3. _____
4. _____

As you look at the summary of common themes, what do you think God is trying to show you about your primary life struggles?

Theme (what God is saying to me)	Related life struggle
Example: *I fear men and erect walls for protection.*	*Trusting men*

FINISHING TOUCH

To return to our *T*, how much trust does forgiveness require? Only enough to roll the stone away. Once we understand that God deliberately allows problems into our lives in order to strengthen our faith, we can trust him no matter what stinky situation we face. If we move the stone away and face the wound or hurt within, we will always encounter his glorious grace. Out of that grace, we reach a marvelous sense of intimacy with him and with our spouse.

Summarize the common themes you identified in the previous Personal Touch by completing the following analysis.

My role	Truth I avoided	Wounded trigger
Example: *Choosing unsafe people to trust*	*Not all people are safe to trust*	*Lack of healthy boundaries with others*

 Briefly review the Touch Up teaching about Mary and Martha and the need for forgiveness. Encourage members to ask God to reveal any further areas of unforgiveness as they prepare for next week's session. Go over the Home Play assignment (see appendix 4 or 5) and pray aloud as you close today's meeting.

2

Openness

Foundation of New Beginnings

TED

IN TOUCH

The area of openness in our marriage has been both difficult and lifesaving. Difficult because when I was growing up, the only one who was allowed to communicate about thoughts, feelings, and opinions was my dad. If I dared to speak, I was yelled at or slapped. I quickly learned to keep everything locked up inside.

My marriage relationship with Dan had three major areas of stress. First, I was emotionally overloaded since I didn't know how to express my needs. When I tried to talk with my husband, he wouldn't give me his full attention. I translated this as "You're not important." If he did respond, he often made a sarcastic comment that wounded my self-worth. Second, our spiritual life was empty. My religious background said God was too important to bother with my concerns.

The Sexy Christians challenge:

allow Christ to bring healing through the hassles.

And if I couldn't talk to him on Sundays, there was no way I would talk with him during the week. Third, I was becoming more and more disconnected from Dan sexually. How could I listen to him at night when he was so uncaring throughout the day? I became cold and emotionally distant, which led my thoughts toward divorce.

God had a plan. He moved some old friends to Oregon so they could present Jesus to my husband and me. I discovered I could talk to God any time I wanted to. I began to learn who I was and that I was valuable enough to communicate. God also allowed us to attend a Marriage Encounter weekend. At this seminar I learned I could—and should—openly express my thoughts and disagreements.

The instructors gave us an assignment that required us to communicate on any nonexplosive topic. I told Dan that talking to him intimidated me. His demeanor and harsh words made the environment unsafe. He had no idea I felt that way.

That single assignment opened the floodgates. I discovered I harbored resentment and anger due to my fears of abandonment and rejection. And Dan learned something valuable too: I needed a safe environment in order to be open about my thoughts and feelings and to continue to grow into who I am in Christ.

Now our marriage is restored and renewed. Emotionally, I am free to express my thoughts, needs, even my disagreements to Dan. What a precious gift! Spiritually, we both desire to know and serve our Lord. His mercies are new every day, and he longs for us to communicate with him so we may continue to grow. Sexually, our desire to please the other first has been awakened. When Dan listens to me during the day, telling me I am valuable, important, and special, I listen to him in our bedroom. He creates an environment of safety, and I grow in openness so I can give myself to him in sexual freedom.

True openness has enhanced our relationship and allowed it to grow in intimacy, trust, and connection.—Ellen

TOUCH DOWN

We have already seen how our level of intimacy is tied directly to our level of relationship with God. Color in the hearts below to show the level of openness you have in various relationships. The shading should range from completely light or not colored at all (closed, impersonal, no communication) to completely dark or filled in (intimate, warm, open communication).

(Your family of origin during childhood)

(Your relationship with God during childhood)

(Your family of origin when you were a teen)

(Your relationship with God during the teen years)

(Your relationship with your spouse
when you got married)

(Your relationship with God when you
and your spouse got married)

(Your relationship with your spouse today)

(Your relationship with God today)

 TOUCH DOWN

Men, you have to admit it. The morning face-scraping routine is a bizarre ritual. You grasp a surgically sharp miniature knife (most now come with multiple blades)

 "Why do we struggle so much to be open and understanding with the person we love most? Why do those wounds and family patterns of the past rise up and make openness such an excruciating choice?"
—*Sexy Christians*

 Welcome members and ask someone to open the session in prayer. Remind the group of the T.O.U.C.H. format. This session (and the next in the twelve-week plan) will focus on *O: openness*. Read the quote from *Sexy Christians* aloud. Ask Ted's question: "Why do we struggle so much to be open and understanding with the person we love most?" Listen with the goal of building relationships, not obtaining a definitive answer.

and, while still half asleep, use it to scrape the hair off your face. Thanks to modern conveniences, it's a fairly safe experience. But things can still get messy every now and then.

One morning as I rounded the corners of my chin, I sliced through an old scar. Within a few seconds blood spread across the sink. The flowing water only made the scene more macabre. Everywhere I looked, I saw blood.

That's when I realized something was causing me to overreact. My pulse was rising; my breathing had become rapid and shallow. *I saw plenty of blood on the battlefield. Why would a simple razor cut on the chin cause me to react so strongly? What's going on inside?*

Have you ever asked yourself a question like that?

Why does that silly thing my spouse does drive me crazy?

Why do I sometimes react so angrily to what my mate says?

Why do little things set me off?

Why do the kids drive me up the wall when I know they are just being kids?

Why do I feel so uneasy when the boss asks me a simple question?

The human mind is an amazing creation. The brain weighs in at only three pounds or about 2 percent of your body weight, but it uses up to 20 percent of the calories you consume. That's a lot of energy. In fact, some guys have used so much energy they've burned the hair right off the top of their heads!

My college majors were mathematics and astrophysics, so I used to think the most complex parts of creation were the galaxies, pulsars, and quasars. But these are simple compared to the human brain. Scientists estimate each brain contains *one hundred billion* neurons or brain cells—the approximate number of stars in our galaxy. But the connections between the neurons (not the neurons themselves) define the brain. On average, each has 10,000 connections.[1] So the average brain has more neurological connections than there are stars in the entire cosmos. Talk about complex!

This helps explain why you can find yourself reacting to the past without knowing why. Our brains don't come into this world fully developed. Instead, we all start out with *implicit memories*.[2] These unconscious factors rely on brain structures intact at birth and available throughout life. We can't recall these memories in the classic sense of the word, but they give us our most foundational feelings. Explicit memories and higher brain functions start developing during our preschool years. But we can still block significant memories if they're overwhelming and filled with terror.[3]

The early years of our lives form the lens through which we perceive the world. Although we receive some of our most fundamental social and emotional lessons during this time, we have little conscious memory of acquiring them. We experience these early lessons as life's givens and rarely question their existence or challenge their validity. We don't normally recognize the fact that they affect and direct our daily perceptions of life and love.

Studies have shown, however, that early experiences can have long-term effects on the way we view life. Recent research reveals the physical and emotional health of men in midlife correlate significantly with their descriptions of the amount of warmth they experienced from their parents thirty-five years before.[4] In other words, *we can react in marriage out of the hurts of our past without realizing it.*

PERSONAL TOUCH

Take some time to consider the early messages your family of origin communicated about sex and sexuality. Think back on your childhood as you respond to each of the following questions.

What are your first memories of your genitals, and how did your family respond to nudity?

Mom: _____

_____

Dad: _____

_____

Siblings: _____

_____

What were the messages your family gave you about sex in your growing-up years?

Mom: _____

_____

Dad: _____

_____

Siblings: _____

_____

How were sexual questions answered or discussed concerning:

your body? _____

_____

where babies come from? _____

_____

self-stimulation? _____

_____

What messages about sex did you receive:

from peers? _____

_____

from your religious training? _____

_____

Briefly summarize any sexual trauma you may have received during your growing-up years.

_____

_____

_____

Share the answers to all of the questions above with your mate and compare your different attitudes and experiences.

 TOUCH DOWN

In God's sovereign love and grace, he brings us into a marriage relationship to throw light on these issues. During the first years of our marriage, I frequently became angry. Diane didn't give up on me, but she wouldn't let me get away with my angry outbursts either. Her tenacity and love finally helped me face my anger. But as I mention in *Sexy Christians*, I couldn't seem to open up to her.

Why not? I deeply loved my wife, but when one of those moments occurred when we could deeply bond as a couple, I instinctively pulled back. Why? And does that have any connection with why I reacted so strongly when I cut my chin?

Again we return to the beginning of life for the answer. The human brain doesn't come into existence fully wired, nor does it develop step-by-step. The right cerebral hemisphere (the part of our brain grounded in sensory or emotional experiences) goes through a sudden growth spurt during the first eighteen months of life.[5]

The right side of our brain appears to contain the organizational framework for a personal emotional self. It also responds to negative emotional stimuli even before we are consciously aware. In other words, unconscious emotional processing based on our past invisibly guards our moment-to-moment thoughts, feelings, and behaviors.[6] The key point: *because the right side of our brain develops first, it organizes*

"They were in trouble—deep trouble—in their relationships and their sexual lives. These were decent folks. They went to church, prayed, and read the latest books on marriage and relationships. But nothing seemed to be working. . . . Without exception their understanding of real intimacy and of their own sexuality was either nonexistent or deeply flawed."
—*Sexy Christians*

and stores many early emotional and social experiences that can emerge later—especially when we are under stress.

PERSONAL TOUCH

Sometimes it's difficult to remember things that happened early in our lives. But as we stop and think, pictures may come to mind. Spend a few minutes recalling your early childhood (years one through ten) by using the timelines below. Re-create the timelines on a larger sheet of paper so there's room to write. On each one, use red ink to place one- or two-word descriptions of times when you faced difficulties or challenges (e.g., early hospitalization, family move, poor school performance). Then use blue ink and add short descriptions of blessings you experienced at those ages (e.g., family dinners, excelling in baseball, best friend).

birth | 1   2   3   4   5   6   7   8   9   10

Now do the same thing on the following timeline of your preteen and teen years.

11   12   13   14   15   16   17   18   19

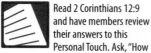

Read 2 Corinthians 12:9 and have members review their answers to this Personal Touch. Ask, "How has God taken your life message and turned it into a *God message* of his grace?" For example: "Because I felt devalued when I was growing up, God has given me compassion and sensitivity to value others the way he values me." Adapt it as necessary.

Finally, use black ink to denote lessons learned or beliefs formed through the experiences listed. (For example: "If I'm smart, they'll love me." "Hard work pays off." "Authority figures will hurt me.")

TOUCH DOWN

I was sitting in a neuroscience lecture presented by Dr. Louis Cozolino, one of the world's experts in the rapidly growing field of neuroscience and an engaging, articulate speaker. I was expecting a cloud of obscure terminology with little application to real life and the couples I counsel. But that day his words seemed to have been uniquely anointed and applied directly to me.

I was fascinated as Dr. Cozolino explained that 70 percent of the time, mothers hold their newborns on their left side. I had seen Diane follow that same pattern with our children—a moving but strange scene for someone like me who grew up in a home with little warmth and attachment. I remember thinking, *Diane is so foolish—cute, but foolish—to do all that baby talk with our kids. I mean, come on, they can't even talk back.*

The pieces began to fall into place as Dr. Cozolino explained that mothers instinctively hold their children in their left arm so they can access the right side of the brain. As Mom soothes her child, she literally uses her voice as a scaffold around which the child's rapidly growing brain can structure itself. The mother's caring tone and touch give the child the critical skills of self-soothing and dealing with stressful situations. Tears came to my eyes as I realized anew what an incredible gift my wife has been to our family.

Next the neuroscientist gave an example of a six-month-old having his messy diapers changed by Mom or Dad. Dr. Cozolino explained what would happen if the parent who changed the diaper was angry, a perfectionist, or obsessive-compulsive. "The uptight parent communicates a message of shame to the child's mind before that child can distinguish the difference between actions and identity. *That is why some individuals live with a haunting sense of shame.*"[7]

There in the midst of that lecture, I had a worship service. I'm sure the other clinicians thought I had gone crazy, but I didn't care. Suddenly I realized why I had seen individuals who loved God with all their heart but still struggled. They prayed, read their Bible, and attended every class possible but couldn't seem to escape the haunting sense of shame within. The problem was not a lack of willpower but a deep inner wound. Only God could help them work through such extreme pain. In order to do it, they would have to access their unconscious thought processes. That's a specialty of the Holy Spirit.

So why did I react so strongly to the blood dripping from my chin? God gradually provided the answer as he moved me toward wholeness. First, I had to realize Diane was indeed Christ's instrument of healing and listen to her words about my anger. Deep inside I knew she was right. I asked God to help me understand the anger's source. *I had to open my heart so my head could get straight.*

As I prayed, a long-ago comment from my mother popped in from my subconscious. She was vigorously washing my face as only a mother can. She made an offhand comment about the extensive scar under my chin. Tears welled up in her eyes as she told me that when I was a toddler, my drunken stepfather grabbed me by the heels and swung me around the room. In his intoxicated state, he lost his grip. I went flying through the air and smashed chin first into a brick fireplace. The accident literally peeled my chin wide open. The blood, screaming, and emotional exchange between my mom and stepdad were horrific.

It all began to make sense. No, I couldn't blame my step-father for my angry attitudes. The Holy Spirit wouldn't give me that excuse. Instead, he was helping me to understand the battle that raged within.

Do you know how it feels to have a parent, relative, teacher, coach, drunken stepfather, or other authority figure drop you? Especially if you don't realize what has happened, this event can affect you for life. Like me, you can find yourself sabotaging your closest relationships. What others consider normal seems like hell to you. Things they can do easily take a huge effort for you to accomplish. That was why I kept crying out to God whenever I reacted angrily to my wife and couldn't figure out why.

My implicit memories of early childhood were distorting my perspective. Would I open my life to God's grace and my heart to the Holy Spirit's work in my head?

PERSONAL TOUCH

Think back to your childhood. First, write down one of your most pleasant memories of a positive interaction with someone else.

_____

_____

_____

Next, give a brief personal example from your life when someone—especially someone you trusted—*dropped* you physically, emotionally, or sexually.

_____

_____

_____

Write a few sentences or draw a picture to describe how the *drop* affects you today.

This activity marks the end of part A for groups following the twelve-week plan. Remind members of God's authority. He allowed—but did not cause—the *dropped* moments members named here. Distribute index cards and ask them to list these again. Designate a table or footstool as an altar and then ask members to bring their cards to the altar and symbolically release the *drops* to God. Point out the Home Play assignment and close in prayer.

TOUCH UP

Allow me to introduce you to a dear friend—a little-known character in the Old Testament who has been part of God's healing process in my heart and marriage. You run into his story in the second book of Samuel.

The king asked, "Is there no one still left of the house of Saul to whom I can show God's kindness?"

Ziba answered the king, "There is still a son of Jonathan; he is crippled in both feet."

"Where is he?" the king asked.

Ziba answered, "He is at the house of Makir son of Ammiel in Lo Debar."

So King David had him brought from Lo Debar, from the house of Makir son of Ammiel. When Mephibosheth son of Jonathan, the son of Saul, came to David, he bowed down to pay him honor. David said, "Mephibosheth!"

"Your servant," he replied.

"Don't be afraid," David said to him, "for I will surely show you kindness for the sake of your father Jonathan. I will restore to you all the land that belonged to your grandfather Saul, and you will always eat at my table."

Mephibosheth bowed down and said, "What is your servant, that you should notice a dead dog like me?" . . .

Then Ziba said to the king, "Your servant will do whatever my lord the king commands his servant to do." So Mephibosheth ate at David's table like one of the king's sons.

2 Samuel 9:3–8, 11

Mephibosheth. How would you like to have a name like that? He was in line for the throne of Israel until his father, Jonathan, died in combat with the Philistines. Right then God did something only he could do. He reached right over Mephibosheth and selected an unknown as king.

Some time before that, God had come to the prophet Samuel, who was weeping over the spiritual disaster King Saul had become, and told him about the little shepherd boy, David, whom he had chosen as the next king (1 Sam. 16:1). But David's own father, Jesse, considered him so worthless he didn't think of having him anywhere near when Samuel came to anoint Saul's successor.

That fact explains a great deal about David's heart for worship. When God takes you from the *gutter-most* to the uttermost in life, you don't act as if you deserve the position. You're so thankful that you look for ways to bless others. We see David's heart at its best when he asks, "Who is left in the household of Saul to whom I can show God's kindness?" His generosity is especially amazing since King Saul spent over a decade hunting David down. Yet here David seeks a way to bless Saul's grandchildren. When he commands his servant to find Mephibosheth, the language is forceful: "Go snatch him out of there!"[8]

In essence God gives this same commandment to the Holy Spirit with respect to both your life and mine. It doesn't matter if you grew up in the perfect Christian home or came to Christ after a life of drugs and desperation. We are all born with the stuff for relational destruction. Marriage helps you confront that fact at close range. When you say hurtful things to your spouse, you both catch a glimpse of what's hidden deep inside.

Mephib ended up in a place called Lo Debar, which means a barren place of desolation and silence. Mephib sits there, convinced that absolutely no one cares about him. Suddenly, he hears a knock on the door. "Who is it?"

"Ziba," the man replies.

"I don't know any Ziba. Go away!"

After a pause, Mephib hears another knock on his door. Now he is irritated. "Who is it?"

"Ziba," he hears again.

"What do you want?" he fires back.

"The king has need of you!"

In a poignant picture of what Christ later did for us, King David has Mephib carried to his palace (2 Sam. 9:5). If you decided to follow Christ, it wasn't because you figured it all out and independently made the decision. God gave you the ability to make the decision; he carried you there (Eph. 2:4–10). Having a great marriage and sex life together is not something we can pull off by ourselves either. We need God to carry us there.

TOUCH UP

David brings Mephib to the palace, but God is far from finished with his work in Mephib's life. Jonathan's son has escaped Lo Debar but is battling something: *he can't walk!* How did he end up in such a crippled condition? Well if you read 2 Samuel 4:4, you will discover something that may not surprise you: *Mephib was dropped.*

The news that David was the new king hit Israel's culture like a tsunami. In the ancient Near East, if you became king and your father hadn't been king before you, you had to hunt down and slaughter every member of the previous royal

This activity marks the start of part B for the twelve-week plan. Contact two group members ahead of time and ask them to prepare to share their Lo Debars and how God carried them out. As time allows, encourage other group members to tell their stories. Keep the focus positive and hopeful. Remain sensitive to the fact that some members may be in a Lo Debar now.

Your Lo Debars

List at least two Lo Debars where you have been, either on your own or in your marriage.	How did God lift you out of that situation?

family. Since Mephib's nanny didn't know David's heart, she grabbed the little boy and ran. In her haste, she dropped him, crippling him for life. Like many of us, Mephib struggled in the present because of a past event.

Since we already know God can redeem those *dropped* moments, we dare not miss one final element. While Mephib was down in Lo Debar thinking no one knew or cared about his struggles, the king was preparing a place for him at the banquet table. No, it wasn't a back corner or a seat in the losers' section. It was a place of honor, blessing, and love.

My friend, Christ is preparing a place for *you* at a table set for only two. Only a sovereign, majestic God could pull this off: a unique place beside him for each of us. And he has already done it for you! John 14 reminds us of Christ's promise:

> My Father's house has many rooms. If that were not true, would I have told you that I'm going to prepare a place for you? If I go to prepare a place for you, I will come again. Then I will bring you into my presence so that you will be where I am.
>
> John 14:2–3 GW

PERSONAL TOUCH

Our past sometimes makes it difficult to imagine a place Jesus would set just for us. Use the following space to draw a picture of your family of origin sitting around the table you had back then. What shape was the table, and where did your family members sit? How often did you eat meals together? Explain your picture to your spouse and share any memories, both precious and painful.

Spend some time discussing the pictures group members drew and their experiences with family dinners. If time allows, ask them to describe how those dinners compare with the ones they have today.

TOUCH DOWN

As we pointed out in *Sexy Christians*, every married couple eventually runs into the wall of a stalemate. It shows up when we argue over irresolvable issues. The stalemate underlies the arguments over what actually happened or who's right and who's wrong, and the real issue is whose definition of reality will triumph. It shows up when we react in anger or frustration to our mate's lack of affirmation or acceptance. We want to avoid the pain that having a great marriage requires, so we find ourselves stuck in stalemate mode.

Apart from Christ's grace and acceptance, these are insurmountable obstacles. He alone can define our reality. He alone will always accept and affirm us. He alone can give us the courage to deal with the pain—and the openness—required for a great marriage.

But this is not the end of the story—Mephib's or ours. At some point, no matter how hard we've been dropped, we have to *get up off the floor*. We must realize the danger of allowing the implicit memories of our past to control our present potential.

I could have spent the rest of my life blaming a drunken stepfather. I could have lain on the floor of my situation, angry about the way he dropped me. I could have continued to flare up in anger. And eventually, I would have killed our sex life and marriage. The eroding anger within would have kept me sliding deeper into the addictions of my past. None of those look like good options, do they?

Getting up off the floor was tough. It took everything I had to face the pain and patterns of my past. At times it felt as though I was crawling hand over hand. Just when you're ready to take your place at the table God has prepared, Satan will unleash his most devastating attacks. But once you have a seat in the place of God's grace, you will look back and realize no demon in hell can keep you and your marriage from God's blessing if only you *get up off the floor*.

PERSONAL TOUCH

Issues not dealt with in our past can rise up to cripple us in the present. Of the list below, check any that may be blocking your intimacy with your spouse:

☐ unresolved anger
☐ having to be right
☐ demanding, self-focused sexual behavior
☐ out-of-control issues with shopping or finances
☐ out-of-control issues with food
☐ out-of-control issues with sex
☐ out-of-control issues with drugs or alcohol
☐ out-of-control issues with gambling
☐ lack of intimacy with God

Now think about your marriage. What would *getting up off the floor* look like for you? How would your actions and attitudes change? Write words or phrases in each column to help describe the changes God could bring about.

Getting Up Off the Floor

On the floor: attitudes and actions	Off the floor: attitudes and actions

"When we don't deal with the trauma we've experienced, we have trouble getting up off the floor. In addition, we have a tendency to become very impulsive in our approach to life. . . . If you aren't regularly enjoying God, you will be profoundly vulnerable to the temptation to medicate your pain by acting impulsively."
—*Sexy Christians*

Write *Impulsive Actions* on your whiteboard or butcher paper. Read the preceding quote aloud and explain that we often deal with pain by self-medicating through impulsivity. Discuss and list some examples of impulsive actions (i.e., overspending, binge eating) and how these pull us away from openness and intimacy. Ask the Holy Spirit's guidance to know how personal the discussion should become.

Prepare for a time of worship as a group. Be creative: play one or more songs from a praise CD, serve communion, read a passage of Scripture, or have a member share in song. Make sure whatever you decide to do reflects God's work in group members' lives and serves as an expression of his love.

FINISHING TOUCH

Our past woundedness impacts nothing else as deeply as it does our sexual relationships as husband and wife. Remember? Intimacy means *being close and uncomfortable* with the person you love. In our most intimate relationships, uncomfortable issues like wounds from being dropped in the past, masks we wear, or the tension of unfulfilled dreams all tend to surface. These things can cause us to feel as crippled emotionally and spiritually as Mephib was physically. But Christ will cover us if we willingly take a seat at the place he has set for us.

If you had walked into King David's dining hall and seen Mephib sitting at the table with royalty, you would never have seen his handicap. The tablecloth of David's grace covered him beautifully.

There were other times when I cut my chin shaving, but eventually the anger within was healed by God's gracious hand. He graciously allowed me to face my pain and move into openness with God and with Diane. When it last happened, God used the moment to remind me of how Christ's shed blood has covered and is healing me.

You see, when you allow Christ to carry you, he makes up for all the wounds of the past. He will never drop you. When you take a seat at his table, his kindness not only covers but changes you as well. And eventually, he heals all the crippled places in your life.

What do you think your place *as a couple* looks like at Christ's table? Let your imagination run wild and draw a picture of it in the space that follows. If you wish, draw the picture together on a larger piece of paper and share it with your children.

3

Understanding

Key to Refining Our Hearts

DIANE

IN TOUCH

Randy and I met at a college group, dated for a month, and became engaged. We believed we were meant to be together. Immediately we began premarital counseling. After we took a personality test, the pastor informed us of some red flags. My results showed a tendency to be strong and assertive; Randy was more passive. Our pastor predicted real problems if we failed to deal with this issue.

We didn't like his conclusions, so we made an appointment with a professional Christian counselor. Before that appointment, Randy admitted he had been diagnosed with OCD (Obsessive-Compulsive Disorder). He had taken himself off his medication and was trying hard to act normally.

Distraught, I canceled the engagement. What had happened to my perfect fiancé?

The Sexy Christians challenge:

allow God to change you through your mate.

The counselor confirmed we could not ignore the OCD. In order to pursue marriage, we would have to not only work through that issue but also address the fact that we were both Type A perfectionists. The lights were flashing: Warning! Disastrous marriage ahead!

The counselor emphasized that we needed to understand one another and learn to communicate honestly. Since we hadn't practiced those skills in our families of origin, we were both on a huge learning curve.

The counselor didn't sugarcoat our potential problems. We realized we would have to do things differently than most couples if we were going to commit to marriage. We would have to be honest with each other and learn the skills to deal with Randy's OCD. And he would have to stay on his medication.

After a lot of work with the counselor, we were re-engaged nine months later and married two years from the time we met. We credit our four wonderful years of marriage to a number of things. We allowed many people—including professionals—to speak into our lives. We have continued to grow by being a part of a small group that keeps us accountable.

We also made a decision to work toward understanding the other person's perspective. We try hard to show respect for each other's opinions. I've learned to listen and not jump to conclusions. Randy's honesty helped me realize that sometimes he responds out of his OCD rather than anything I've done.

God has truly blessed our openness, honesty, and all the work we did to walk in health. Counseling helped us realize the OCD would not change—but we could learn ways to cope. Our commitment to understand one another and work on our issues as a team has produced a strong marriage.—Beth

TOUCH DOWN

For our fortieth anniversary, Ted whisked me away to a romantic week on a remote island near Fiji. Dining outdoors as we watched the beautiful island sunsets and showering in a private outdoor shower renewed our desire.

Have a pack of dot stickers available for use during this session. Open in prayer and ask the group to brainstorm issues that should be discussed before marriage. Record the list on your whiteboard or butcher paper. Ask each person to place a dot beside the three most important issues. Circle the three to five items that receive the most dots and discuss them.

One afternoon, we launched a kayak to a private beach we had reserved on the other side of the island. We rolled in the surf and re-created our own updated version of *From Here to Eternity* as we made new—and passionate—memories together.

PERSONAL TOUCH

Write down the answers to these questions and discuss them with your mate.

When was the last time you did something as a couple that brought about a passionate memory you both enjoy rehearsing?

_____

_____

_____

_____

What passionate memory do you treasure most?

_____

_____

_____

_____

What dream getaway would you like to plan?

_____

_____

_____

_____

Without asking couples to share explicit memories, have them discuss some of their most romantic times together. Ask questions such as:

Does your romantic memory involve travel?

How did you find time to make this memory?

What advice would you give to other couples about creating memories?

How can we as a group help in this process?

Encourage an open time of sharing and celebration as couples.

TOUCH DOWN

Two days before our planned departure from the island, we noticed a husband and wife who looked totally out of place. Because this resort limited accommodations to less than twenty couples, new arrivals were obvious. These two were especially so because they sported heavy sweaters and warm slacks. We began a conversation out of curiosity and learned the two had left chilly Chicago for this tropical honeymoon. The airline had lost their luggage, so here on a private island with no available shops, they were stuck with inappropriate attire.

What a horrible way to start married life! I thought. Then it dawned on me: most of us start marriage just like that. Unlike Beth and Randy, who realized they had baggage to deal with before marriage, most of us don't have the luxury of knowing baggage exists. We face moments of surprise and disappointment when the delayed baggage unexpectedly appears. It can come in the form of anger, selfishness, unreasonable expectations, and so forth. Most of it comes because, like Randy, we try to present our best selves during the dating process. But that can only last so long. Eventually, all couples find themselves in the marriage crucible that brings out their best or worst.

On your wedding day, you assumed you were marrying the perfect person. And guess what? You did!

 PERSONAL TOUCH

At a particular point in your relationship, you began to realize your spouse was "the one." Make a list of the qualities and events God used (whether you knew it or not) to help you realize he was drawing the two of you together. (For example: intelligence, strong faith, love of children; or spilling my Coke on him at the restaurant, borrowing his pen, moving into the apartment next door to her.)

_____

_____

_____

_____

"You and your mate did not meet by accident. A sovereign, passionate, and romantic God was at work in your lives long before you first noticed one another. . . . Call me a ridiculous romantic, a heretic, whatever. Each of us has free will, but God, in the mystery of his sovereignty, brought you and your spouse together. When a couple truly realizes that fact, it changes everything."—*Sexy Christians*

TOUCH UP

The next letter in our T.O.U.C.H acrostic is *U* for *Understanding*. That should be an easy concept; we use the term almost every day. But true understanding, especially within marriage, doesn't come naturally. As we pointed out in *Sexy Christians*, we often try to relate to our spouse from the perspective of the Golden Rule ("do unto others as you would have them do unto you") rather than the Ephesians Rule (from chapter 5, which teaches that husbands must *love* their wives and wives must *respect* their husbands). Attempts to understand from our own perspective often end in disaster.

God does not set out to make his children comfortable. Instead, he works to make us look like him, to transform us into his image. "And so we are transfigured much like the Messiah, our lives gradually become brighter and more beautiful as God enters our lives and we become like him" (2 Cor. 3:18 Message). How does he accomplish this? How does he help us grow in understanding ourselves, our spouse, and our God?

When we say "I do," we are thrown into God's marriage tumbler. He uses the rough edges and differences we each bring to the relationship as abrasive compounds that make us shine. God uses the things that irritate us as we knock against each other to polish and brighten our lives. It takes time and effort to produce the beautiful marriage we all desire. Often, we long to escape the pain and pressure of the tumbler. Divorce may seem like the only way out.

In the fifth chapter of the Song of Songs, the pain escalates during a conversation between Shulamith and Solomon. For some reason, things have come to a head as Shulamith rejects Solomon's romantic overtures with excuses similar to the modern-day "headache."

What baggage delay suddenly shows up in their relationship? We can only speculate, but if we look carefully, we can see some red flags during their courtship. In the opening chapter, we read the following statement from Shulamith: "Do not stare at me because I am swarthy, for the sun has

Earlier, couples shared stories about how they met. Now encourage them to share some positive qualities that made them realize their spouse was *the one*. Have group members take turns listing two of these special qualities on the whiteboard or butcher paper. If appropriate, lead members to discuss any patterns they notice. This marks the end of part A for the twelve-week plan.

burned me. My mother's sons were angry with me; they made me caretaker of the vineyards, but I have not taken care of my own vineyard" (Song of Songs 1:6 NASB).

Shulamith is self-conscious about her appearance and refers to her brothers' mistreatment. Because they made her work hard, she neglected her self-care. Now in the king's palace, where she had hoped to find relief from the pain of her past, she instead feels harsh, condescending stares from the other women. Could it be that these same insecurities surfaced when she rejected her lover and caused him to turn away from their bedchamber?

Insecurities and hurts from our past are some of the rough edges God intends to smooth out. By chapter 8, some healing has apparently entered Shulamith's life. A family gathering at the palace includes her entire dysfunctional family. Her brothers taunt and tease her about her flat chest and question if she was a virgin during her courtship. These words transport her to a painful childhood: "We have a little sister, and she has no breasts; what shall we do for our sister on the day when she is spoken for? . . . If she is a door, we will barricade her with planks of cedar" (Song of Songs 8:8–9 NASB).

Shulamith demonstrates a new sense of self-assertiveness as she stands up to her brothers. She responds with maturity, "I was a wall, and my breasts are like towers" (Song of Songs 8:10). What brought her to this new place of wisdom and transformation?

Three things shaped her new polished presence: understanding the hurts from her family of origin, understanding herself through her mate's unconditional love, and turning her understanding into actions that reflected her true identity. We'll spend the rest of the chapter exploring each of these in turn.

PERSONAL TOUCH

You and your spouse have special memories together, but you also remember times of pain. One of the ways we can understand our spouse is by understanding his or her experience of a painful situation or circumstance.

Use this space to draw a picture to represent the most hurtful experience in your marriage so far.

Next, write three words to describe how you felt when it occurred.

_____

Write three more words to describe how you feel about this experience today.

_____

If you can, share these experiences and feelings with your spouse. Remember not to judge or criticize your mate's feelings but to listen attentively. Afterward, pray together as you ask God to redeem the pain and use this exercise to help you grow together in understanding.

 TOUCH DOWN

Let's dig a little deeper as we apply the process to our lives. First, we need to *understand the hurts from our family of origin*. There are no perfect families, and we are not encouraging you to blame your parents for all your

 "Intimacy is not *being close and comfortable*. That is one of the great myths being taught in the world (even the Christian world) today. Intimacy is not *learning the latest sexual technique or fad* either. According to what we see in Scripture, true biblical intimacy is *developing the ability to be uncomfortably close and vulnerable with another imperfect human*."
—*Sexy Christians*

problems. But most of us don't understand the power of our family's imprint upon our lives.

A cartoon from Mother Goose & Grimm says it best. The first frame shows the dog Grimm with this caption: "Y'know . . . running away from home would be a lot more fun. . . ." The second frame shows him leashed to his doghouse with it bumping along behind as he runs, ". . . if I didn't always have to take home with me!"

Like it or not, we all take our home with us no matter how much we run from it or vow we will never be like our mom or dad. Certain neurological freeways are carved into our brains by the time we leave home. This explains why we can consider something to be *normal* that is actually *dysfunctional*. Like Shulamith's, our thinking has become conditioned. Her previous conditioning to mistreatment caused her to act like a victim. She thought everyone was out to get her whether it was the other women in the palace or Solomon himself.

Examining the past helps us understand the patterns we need to change. Instead of blaming our parents, we want to boldly reclaim what God had in mind when he originally created us. I was aware that Ted, raised by an alcoholic mother and seven stepfathers, brought plenty of baggage into our marriage. I had proof when he took the inventory you will take in a few minutes. His scores were extremely unhealthy: a 1–2, which measured how disengaged and rigid his family was. Addictive behavior is prominent in families that display no relationship (disengaged) and many rules (rigid). Ted's scores held no big surprises.

What did surprise me, however, was this: I scored the same as my husband! I had anticipated at least a 6 or even a 7 since my parents stayed married for more than fifty years until death parted them. There was no alcohol or violence in our home, yet I had the same score as Ted, whose home contained both in abundance. Why?

I then began to realize that the perfectionism, rules, and lack of emotional closeness I experienced had affected me in a similar way as the hurts from Ted's family of origin. I too had brought dysfunctions into our marriage that became obstacles to the intimacy God intended for our lives.

After that inventory, I immediately made changes. I knew whatever issues I failed to confront would cause problems not only for my marriage but for the next generation. God tells us, "I am God, your God, and I'm a most jealous God. I hold parents responsible for any sins they pass on to their children to the third, and yes, even to the fourth generation. But I'm lovingly loyal to the thousands who love me and keep my commandments" (Deut. 5:9–10 Message).

It's never too late to repent and change generational curses. When you make those changes, God's blessing—far more powerful than any curse—can extend to a thousand generations. But where do you start? How do you make those changes?

You start by eliminating denial. When I thought of my family of origin as normal, I lived in a state of denial. Beverly Hubble Tauke powerfully describes that condition: "Denial of personal history is somewhat like a self-inflicted frontal lobotomy. Truth squelching deadens our mental ability to scrutinize, measure, and evaluate experiences that have wired our personal perceptions, expectations, emotions, reactions, choices and relationships."[1]

An objective tool like the inventory that follows helps cut through those warped perceptions and denials. Ultimately, it helps you understand your family of origin.

PERSONAL TOUCH The following inventory is the same one Ted and I took long ago. I encourage you to answer the questions and examine your family of origin. Follow the directions about how to add your scores and transfer the total.

Be careful when you transfer your total results to the next diagram. It should look something like this.

If you scored a total of 55 for cohesion, put a 4 on the bottom blank near the word *cohesion*.

Faces II: Family Version

David H. Olson, Joyce Portner & Richard Bell

1	2	3	4	5
Almost Never	Once in Awhile	Sometimes	Frequently	Almost Always

Describe the family you grew up in:

_____ 1. Family members were supportive of each other during difficult times.

_____ 2. In our family, it was easy for everyone to express his/her opinion.

_____ 3. It was easier to discuss problems with people outside the family than with other family members.

_____ 4. Each family member had input regarding major family decisions.

_____ 5. Our family gathered together in the same room.

_____ 6. Children had a say in their discipline.

_____ 7. Our family did things together.

_____ 8. Family members discussed problems and felt good about the solutions.

_____ 9. In our family, everyone went his/her own way.

_____ 10. We shifted household responsibilities from person to person.

_____ 11. Family members knew each other's close friends.

_____ 12. It was hard to know what the rules were in our family.

_____ 13. Family members consulted other family members on personal decisions.

_____ 14. Family members said what they wanted.

_____ 15. We had difficulty thinking of things to do as a family.

_____ 16. In solving problems, the children's suggestions were followed.

_____ 17. Family members felt very close to each other.

_____ 18. Discipline was fair in our family.

_____ 19. Family members felt closer to people outside the family than to other family members.

_____ 20. Our family tried new ways of dealing with problems.

_____ 21. Family members went along with what the family decided to do.

_____ 22. In our family, everyone shared responsibilities.

_____ 23. Family members liked to spend their free time with each other.

_____ 24. It was difficult to get a rule changed in our family.

_____ 25. Family members avoided each other at home.

_____ 26. When problems arose, we compromised.

_____ 27. We approved of each other's friends.

_____ 28. Family members were afraid to say what was on their minds.

_____ 29. Family members paired up rather than do things as a total family.

_____ 30. Family members shared interests and hobbies with each other.

Directions for Obtaining Circumplex Type Score

For Cohesion:
1. Sum items 3, 9, 15, 19, 25, and 29.
2. Subtract that figure from 36.
3. Sum all other odd numbers *plus* item 30.
4. Add the figures from Step 2 and Step 3 to obtain a total *cohesion* score.

For Adaptability:
1. Sum items 24 and 28.
2. Subtract that figure from 12.
3. Sum all other even numbers *except* item 30.
4. Add the figures from Step 2 and Step 3 to obtain a total *adaptability* score.

Source: D. H. Olsen, C. S. Russell, and D. H. Sprenkle, *Circumplex Model: Systemic Assessment and Treatment of Families* (New York: Haworth, 1988). Used by permission.

Faces II: Linear Scoring & Interpretation

Cohesion			Adaptability			Family Type		
8	80	Very Connected	8	70	Very Flexible	8		Balanced
	74			65				
7	73		7	64		7		
	71			55				
6	70	Connected	6	54	Flexible	6		Moderately Balanced
	65			50				
5	64		5	49		5		
	60			46				
4	59	Separated	4	45	Structured	4		Mid-Range
	55			43				
3	54		3	42		3		
	51			40				
2	50	Disengaged	2	39	Rigid	2		Extreme
	35			30				
1	34		1	29		1		
	15			15				

__ Cohesion + __ Adaptability   __/2 = Type

If you score a 30 on adaptability, put a 2 in the blank next to *adaptability*.

Then add your numbers and divide by two. For example: 4 + 2 = 6, divided by 2 is 3. Put your final number in the blank: 6/2 = 3 Type.

If you scored 3, you would be in the mid-range.

Next, see the Linear Scoring and Interpretation diagram to understand what this type shows about your family of origin.

Notice that the white area on the next page correlates to the top area (8–7–6) on this page where the Balanced Family Types (8–7–6) are reflected in the center. On the next page, mid-range Family Types (5–3) are shaded gray, and the Extreme Family Types (2–1) are shown in the black area.

Couple & Family Map

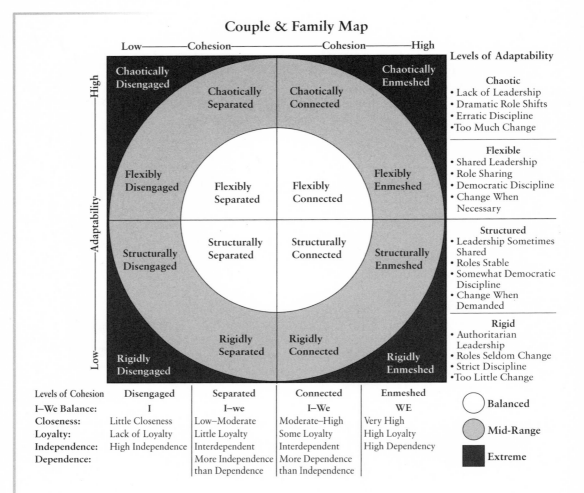

Low—————Cohesion—————————Cohesion————High

Levels of Cohesion	Disengaged	Separated	Connected	Enmeshed
I–We Balance:	I	I–we	I–We	WE
Closeness:	Little Closeness	Low–Moderate	Moderate–High	Very High
Loyalty:	Lack of Loyalty	Little Loyalty	Some Loyalty	High Loyalty
Independence:	High Independence	Interdependent	Interdependent	High Dependency
Dependence:		More Independence than Dependence	More Dependence than Independence	

○ Balanced
◯ Mid-Range
■ Extreme

Levels of Adaptability

Chaotic
• Lack of Leadership
• Dramatic Role Shifts
• Erratic Discipline
• Too Much Change

Flexible
• Shared Leadership
• Role Sharing
• Democratic Discipline
• Change When Necessary

Structured
• Leadership Sometimes Shared
• Roles Stable
• Somewhat Democratic Discipline
• Change When Demanded

Rigid
• Authoritarian Leadership
• Roles Seldom Change
• Strict Discipline
• Too Little Change

TOUCH DOWN

Don't get discouraged if you scored 1–2; remember, those were our families' scores. But something amazing took place. As Ted and I discussed our results and became intentional about changing our family patterns, powerful things happened.

We took time to work through our issues and much of the baggage we brought into our marriage. A few years later, we hesitantly asked our children to take this same test. We couldn't believe it. They each gave their family of origin a final score of 6. In one generation our family had gone from a 1–2 to a 6.

You may wonder what Ted and I did to obtain a large change in a short time. First, we discussed our scores. If possible, examine any questions that yielded low scores and brainstorm about ways to make changes.

Ted and I realized that in order to become more connected than our families of origin, we needed fewer rules and more opportunities for relationship. We spent nights reading and discussing books the kids chose. We asked open-ended questions at dinner like, "On a scale of one to ten, rate your day and explain why you chose the number you did." We made family times (such as game night) a priority and, although Ted had a busy pastor's schedule, we consistently tucked the children in bed and prayed with them together.

PERSONAL TOUCH

What can you do to promote more engagement between family members? List some ways to connect. Circle those you want to work on this week. If you have no children, list ways to connect with your extended family.

1. _____

2. _____

3. _____

4. _____

5. _____

Ted and I also realized we had to model more connectedness and intimacy in our own relationship as an example for our children. Having date nights away from the kids, praying together as husband and wife, and ministering together provided healthy patterns they've now implemented in their

This marks the beginning of part B for the twelve-week plan. Part of coming to understand ourselves is understanding the pain of our past. Prepare in advance for this session by asking one couple to share how pain from the past affected their marriage. If possible, both husband and wife should share. Ask them to conclude with at least one positive thing they see God doing in their marriage today. Thank them for their openness and then pray for the group that God will help them face the pain of their past as they grow in understanding of one another.

"Both genders value connectedness and the communication that goes along with it. The friendship factor—the relationship between the husband and wife—is the overriding factor that determines a couple's satisfaction with their marriage. True biblical intimacy is verbal, physical, relational, and especially spiritual in nature."
—*Sexy Christians*

Ask couples to share some of the ideas for marital connectedness generated here. List them on the whiteboard or butcher paper. Ask if anyone has fulfilled these plans, and agree to hold one another accountable to carry out one or more by the next group session.

own marriages. List some new ways you'd like to connect as a couple:

1. _____

2. _____

3. _____

4. _____

5. _____

Share your answers and agree to follow through with one new way of connecting this week.

TOUCH DOWN

Shulamith not only understands how the pain of her past affects her present, but she also begins to understand herself through her mate's unconditional love, which enables her to see who she really is. As we emphasized in *Sexy Christians*, in your spouse you meet both your patient and your healer.

Solomon is a great example of a healing agent. In his marriage, he consistently validates Shulamith with words and actions. When she is concerned about her dark skin, he addresses her as "fairest among women" (Song of Songs 1:8 NKJV). Although they are strongly attracted to one another, Solomon honors her desire to remain pure until marriage (Song of Songs 2:7). These actions affirm her beauty and worth. Through this constant validation of who she is, Solomon powerfully releases her into her true identity. In this new place of freedom she gains the ability to stand up for herself when her brothers tease her.

Rather than becoming angry and hostile when Shulamith rejects him in chapter 5, Solomon simply leaves and allows her to make the next move. Shulamith may have rationalized her behavior: *He's gone every night! He comes home late. And he constantly puts other people in the kingdom ahead of me*. Her list, like the mental lists we can make of our mate's wrongs, could go on and on.

I hear some of these same laments while counseling. I usually ask the wife what she can do to validate her husband's hard work and help him understand how much she misses him. I also share a revealing interview from a radio program about infidelity. One man expressed that his wife's harsh words made him feel like a failure as a dad and husband. Work was his one place of success; the more his wife complained, the later he stayed at the office. He started an affair with a coworker whom he admitted was not as attractive as his wife but often told him things like, "You're so amazing and gifted on the job. This company would be nothing without you."

This husband and wife had many rough edges. But could the affair have been averted if they had made more efforts to understand one another's needs and struggles?

PERSONAL TOUCH

Here's an opportunity to grow in understanding. Evaluate how well you think you understand your spouse in both words and actions. Check the answers that apply to you in your marriage right now.

- ☐ I emotionally support my spouse.
- ☐ I help create a peaceful, validating atmosphere in our home.
- ☐ My spouse trusts me completely.
- ☐ I have my spouse's welfare in mind when making decisions.
- ☐ I am honest about how I spend money.
- ☐ When I disagree with my spouse, I don't become angry and judgmental.

When you share your answers with your spouse, ask how you can change the areas you could not check. What is something you could do this week that might help you progress in one area? Write it on the next page.

_____

_____

_____

_____

_____

_____

What are some positive things your spouse can say to help
you feel validated, cared for, and understood?

1. _____

2. _____

3. _____

4. _____

5. _____

Share one thing your spouse did in the last week that met
an emotional need. (For example: "He took time to listen to
some fears I had." "She was sensitive and realized my need
for downtime after a busy day.")

List some of your physical and emotional needs and share
them with your spouse.

1. _____

2. _____

3. _____

Write down the most stressful thing you're facing this week.
Then write down some ways your spouse could support you
in getting through it. (For example: "I have a project deadline

soon. My husband can help me by cleaning up after meals or making the kids' lunches."

Stress:

_____

_____

How my spouse can help:

_____

_____

TOUCH DOWN

Once Ted and I recognized the areas of dysfunction in each of our families and understood who we are in Christ through our spouse's affirmation, we (like Shulamith) had to *turn our understanding into actions that reflected our true identity.* We had to act in new ways that reflected our beliefs.

When our daughter was eight, I noticed she expressed some critical, judgmental attitudes. I began to ask myself about the source of this behavior. *Grandma was critical and judgmental, my mom was critical and judgmental, and now my daughter. . . . The problem must have skipped a generation!* Of course it is always easier to notice others' sins than to recognize wrong attitudes and patterns in ourselves.

I had the opportunity to change the negative model passed down through the generations. First, I went to my daughter and repented for transferring the sin. Although the problem didn't start with me, I took responsibility for my part. We also repented to God together and decided to hold each other accountable for the habits we wanted to change. That worked for at least a month, when I found myself slipping back into the negative, critical mode. I was doing exactly what I didn't want to do. The apostle Paul had the same problem: "For what I do is not the good I want to do; no, the evil I do not want to do—this I keep on doing" (Rom. 7:19).

But God, I prayed, *I'm trying so hard not to be negative and critical.* Do you know what he showed me? He does not

Read the Quick Quote aloud. Ask each member in turn to tell about one way their spouse has served as their healer. For example: Allen has consistently affirmed my physical attractiveness although I grew up believing I was homely. Gail values the work I do to support our family. She tells me often how much she appreciates my hard work and professionalism.

"We must understand that our struggles don't all disappear when we come to Christ. They don't all end on our wedding day either. In fact, it seems as though the struggles increase. . . . On the day we marry we also meet our healer, our patient, and our fellow struggler. We meet the one person Christ will uniquely use to bring his transforming power to bear on our lives."
—*Sexy Christians*

73

give grace for the negative—for us *not* to act a certain way or *not* to do a certain thing. Instead he gives us grace to become the people he designed us to be. The Lord led me to Galatians 5:22–23, "But the fruit of the Spirit is love, joy, peace, patience, kindness, goodness, faithfulness, gentleness and self-control." The word *kindness* jumped out of the page as he spoke to my heart, *Diane, you are a gracious woman of God.*

Gracious woman of God. The exact opposite of the way I saw myself, but exactly the way Ted saw me. He had often affirmed me as a beautiful and gracious reflection of Christ, and I knew God was using my husband's understanding to call forth the qualities he had designed me to exhibit all along.

Peter is another biblical example of God's power to change family patterns. His name was Simon, but Jesus called him Peter, *Rock*. When Jesus first called him by his new name, he was anything but stable and solid. When asked if he was one of Jesus's disciples, he cursed and later denied Christ. But Jesus never changed in his affirmation of his wayward disciple's true identity. After the resurrection, he made a special effort to reemphasize Peter's devotion (John 21:15–17). And on the day of Pentecost, a spirit-filled Peter stood before a crowd of more than 3,000 and boldly declared the powerful claims of Christ.

Like Peter, Ted (as he shares in *Sexy Christians*) also struggled with pride as a means of covering his insecurities. His family of origin provided no role model for a humble servant of the Lord. As his wife, I could clearly see his struggle with pride. But I also knew what he had sacrificed and recognized his strengths as a pastor and teacher. God gave me this understanding about my husband, and it was my responsibility to love him into the person God designed him to be. But despite our spouse's affirmations, in order for change to occur, *we had to act on the understanding God had given us.*

As we moved from understanding ourselves to understanding each other to action, Ted and I asked for help from the Holy Spirit. Scripture says he will lead us into all truth (John 16:13). We surrendered our wills and gave him permission to lead us in a new way. I asked him to help me walk in graciousness. Ted renounced his pride and asked the Holy Spirit to help him walk in humility. And God did an amazing work. Whenever I had an opportunity to criticize or judge, I heard his gentle whisper: *Diane, go this way; walk in the spirit of graciousness.* And Ted heard the voice of the Holy Spirit often as he walked away from self-focus and into a love that surpassed all others. Today, although people recognize his wisdom and accomplishments, they also affirm his humility and faithful service to the Lord.

Like Shulamith and like Peter, Ted and I chose to act in ways that reflected the truth. And as we carried out the truth, we watched Christ set free our lives, our marriage, and our family.

PERSONAL TOUCH

What wrong patterns or attitudes do you see that have traveled through the generations of your family? List them here.

_____

_____

_____

Now look at the fruits of the Spirit in Galatians 5:22–23 and the opposite expressions of each virtue shown below. Circle those negative expressions that mesh with the patterns you identified.

Fruit of the Spirit	Opposite expression
Love	Anger, bitterness, hateful or unforgiving spirit
Joy	Depression, discouragement, loneliness
Peace	Anxiety, being easily upset, overattention to unimportant details
Patience	Irritation, frustration, perfectionism
Kindness/Goodness/Gentleness	Critical, harsh, judgmental, or negative spirit
Faithfulness	Fear of risk, inability to trust, unwillingness to commit and follow through
Self-control	Addictions, compulsiveness, impulsiveness, being trapped in out-of-control behaviors

God said:

Diane, you are a gracious woman (kindness).
Peter, you are a Rock (self-control, faithfulness).
Ted, you are a humble servant of the Lord (love, good-
ness).
Shulamith, you are fairest of all (faithful, joyful).

What is God saying to you? Fill in the blanks below with your name and one or more expressions of your identity that he wants to call forth:

_____, you are _____.

Next, repent and renounce the curse that has traveled through your family of origin. In my case, I had to renounce the critical, judgmental, negative spirit that had power in my family and repent for allowing it to control my life. Then thank God for the new name he has given you and ask the Holy Spirit to teach you how to walk as the person God designed you to be. If you understand the power of the patterns of the past and have a new understanding for yourself as you are in Christ, you may want to pray a prayer something like this:

Lord, I renounce the _____
spirit that has had power in my family. I repent for allow-
ing it to control my life. Thank you for the new name you
have given me. Holy Spirit, I don't know how to walk as
_____, *but I give you permission to*
guide me into all truth because I know that is the person you
see me to be. Amen.

Here it may be appropriate for members to share the generational curses they renounced. You may prefer to review biblical examples like Joseph. Regardless, ask each couple to share one marital prayer request. List these where everyone can see them, remind couples of next session's reading and Home Play assignment, and pray for each listed request as you close.

Share with your spouse what you have discovered and pray together that these new patterns will become change agents in your marriage.

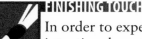
FINISHING TOUCH

In order to experience lasting change, you must be intentional—as Beth and Randy were when they did the hard relational work their counselor assigned. When you choose to understand and take action, you begin to walk in the true image of the person God created you to be. Like Shulamith and Peter, you willingly take that third step and trust the Holy Spirit to show you how to walk into your new identity.

> You were taught, with regard to your former way of life, to put off your old self, which is being corrupted by its deceitful desires; to be made new in the attitude of your minds; and to put on the new self, created to be like God in true righteousness and holiness.
>
> Ephesians 4:22–24

Intimacy begins with an understanding of yourself, your spouse, and your relationship with God. "Faithful is He who calls you, and He also will bring it to pass" (1 Thess. 5:24 NASB). As you open your eyes and hearts to the understanding he gives you, he will bring to pass the true intimacy in marriage you so deeply desire. He will help you become a Sexy Christian.

4

Critical Conversations

Discussions That Matter

T E D

We've been married almost forty-five years, and our ability to reinforce our marriage through critical conversations has grown immensely. During the first ten years of our marriage, our conversations consisted primarily of put-downs and sarcasm by me and angry outbursts by my wife. So how did we get where we are today?

The transformation began with a heart transplant when a friend introduced me to a personal relationship with Jesus. The Holy Spirit started working on my self-centeredness and my need to control. A marriage not grounded in Christ has little chance to succeed, but our newly developing faith helped us commit to staying together and improving our communication. The areas most impacted by our growth were emotional, spiritual, and sexual conversations.

The Sexy Christians challenge:

care enough to talk it out.

Our spiritual conversations changed dramatically and helped us mature enough to grow in the other two areas. It began by developing a pattern of praying together regularly. We also read the Bible together, and occasionally we read a marriage book or couples' devotional together and discuss it. Most recently, we've been sharing our journals.

Our sexual critical conversations also changed as my self-focus decreased. I often crushed my wife's spirit with my harsh words, but then one day the Holy Spirit highlighted a verse from Ephesians: "Do not let any unwholesome talk come out of your mouths, but only what is helpful for building others up according to their needs, that it may benefit those who listen" (Eph. 4:29). I realized that I applied this everywhere in my life except at home. I asked forgiveness and began to look for opportunities to encourage and build up my wife. I saw the connection between the way I met her emotional needs and her receptivity to my sexual advances. We began talking about what pleased us sexually so we could improve. Now in our late sixties, our passion for each other is as strong as it has ever been.

Our emotional critical conversations displayed the greatest challenge and eventually the greatest change. I had grown up believing anger is the only emotion a guy shows. My wife was physically and emotionally abused whenever she verbalized her emotions. In the early years of our marriage we didn't connect at all emotionally. Even after accepting Christ, I had difficulty understanding this area. My wife complained about the emotional distance between us. Finally we talked about how my behavior, words, and body language created an unsafe environment for her. We attended a Marriage Encounter retreat that gave us some practical tools to increase our emotional intimacy.

I believe we'll continue to grow in this area of critical conversations and continue to struggle at times. But God is faithful. If we allow him, he will help us change.—Dan

Read or have a group member read Dan's In Touch testimony. Ask members to share parts of the testimony that relate most to their marriage. What hope do they find here? As time allows, record statements of hope such as "anyone can change" or "sex can improve with age" on the whiteboard or butcher paper.

TOUCH DOWN

Could the day get any more exciting? Diane was finally going to experience my world firsthand! I had recently completed flight training and was about to receive my wings. My class rank was high enough that my superiors granted me the privilege of taking my wife through a simulated takeoff. We would taxi out, line up on the runway, accelerate to a sedate ninety knots, and return to the tarmac. Compared to my vigorous flight training schedule, this sounds simple enough, right?

Wrong. The suiting-up process was hilarious in itself. Diane, always classy and dignified, looked slightly overwhelmed. The flight helmet sat at an awkward angle and the bulky oxygen mask swung back and forth with each step she took. As she struggled forward in her mammoth flight boots, G-suit, harness, and survival vest, her strides were less than graceful. Still, my bride wore her trademark smile along with an obvious delight in my world. That thrilled me.

Amid the normal workplace cacophony of other aircraft starting their engines, zooming overhead, and executing touch-and-goes, I tried to explain my preflight inspection procedures. Although Diane nodded politely after each explanation, I could tell she understood little.

The aircraft captains were grinning like crazy. In those days having a woman on the flight line was a real treat. Intensely focused, I climbed into the front seat. The plane captain was helping Diane navigate the gymnastics of climbing into the rear seat.

After a few minutes I began the radio check, making sure Diane could hear me. She shouted, "How do you adjust this seat?"

"The height adjustment handle is right next to your seat," I told her and continued with my checklist.

That's when it happened. The captain assisting her nearly jumped out of his skin. He shouted something unintelligible and lunged forward. My precious wife was about to kill us all! If she had managed to pull the yellow-and-black-striped ejection lever under her seat, the blast of the rocket would have killed the captain. Next, since I hadn't finished strapping myself in, I would have been killed when my seat automatically fired. Finally, Diane herself would have died after her seat blasted up and out of the aircraft. We all came within seconds of death because we incorrectly assumed we were communicating clearly.

Every couple has *critical conversations* that must take place to keep their marriage from dying a premature death. Even among marriages that last, studies by Dr. Janice Kiecolt-Glaser and Dr. Ronald Glasser show an amazing difference between those who continually argue and those who resolve their differences effectively. Among couples who had been married for an average of forty-two years, those who failed to have critical conversations had far weaker immune systems than those who found ways to resolve their issues well.[1] A weakened immune system leads to poor health, which means critical conversations can be a life-and-death issue.

PERSONAL TOUCH

Often patterns from the past can hinder critical conversations between husband and wife. We see wrong responses modeled in our family of origin or we react from our own insecurities rather than responding appropriately to our spouse. We've designed the following exercise to help you identify your attitudes and behaviors that may make marital communication difficult.

Ask the Holy Spirit's help to recognize and circle those that apply to you.

I need to be right.
I blame my spouse or circumstances for the problem.
I focus only on my needs.
I attempt to control or manipulate to get my way.
I withdraw physically or emotionally from my spouse.
I become defensive or make excuses.
I have angry outbursts or responses.
Other: _____

Confess to God and your spouse the areas you've identified.

Next, think back on a recent conversation when you used any of these attitudes or behaviors. Identify which one(s) and briefly describe how (and if) your family of origin modeled this behavior.

_____

_____

_____

_____

Think through that same recent conversation and come up with other, healthier ways you could have approached it. Write those new ideas here and share them with your spouse. (Examples: ask questions, ask for clarification, write out my feelings, and share when emotions subside.)

_____

_____

_____

_____

"Within the context of marriage, our self-centered and selfish attitudes become obvious. We have the choice of remaining as we are and watching our sexual relationship lose its passion and power or following God's plan: death to our selfish desires and new life that renews intimacy and recharges the sex life."
—*Sexy Christians*

 TOUCH DOWN

The near-death scene on the airfield has replayed many times in our more than forty years of marriage when misunderstood words launched us in crazy directions. Without critical conversations, real marital intimacy—not to mention survival—is impossible.

In my attempts to communicate clearly and lovingly with my wife, I've watched myself pass through four distinct stages. The first stage is *foolishness*. Because I've said something, I can foolishly assume Diane understands it. I communicate easily with the guys in my small group or at the gym, but sometimes I'm a certified fool who forgets that Diane comes not from another planet but an entirely different world.

Ask a group member to read the preceding quote aloud. Ask members to think about their first year of marriage and the current one. On a scale of 1–10 (1 completely self-focused, 10 completely focused on the other), how would they rate their selfishness during both years? Have members share responses aloud. Do not attempt to solve problems but help couples recognize the need for critical communication.

"Over the years I've learned the joys and the problems we experience in our marriage usually arise from the same fact: *we are so different.* Each of us has qualities that make us fundamentally, foundationally, radically different from one another." —*Sexy Christians*

This always leads to stage two, *frustration.* I deeply desire sexual and emotional closeness with my wife, yet things can turn sideways within seconds. *Maybe things will be fixed if I say it again. Or maybe if I say it loudly. . . . Yeah, she'll get it then.* Either approach ends with me sleeping on the couch.

The couch experiences lead to the third stage, *focused attention. Hey, I fly jet planes; I can figure out how to talk to my wife. Surely there's a checklist somewhere to show me how to do this.* Focused attention got me off the couch but never helped me reach my goal of real intimacy.

This brought me full circle to a dilemma called *total frustration. Getting smarter doesn't cut it. Trying harder doesn't either.* What could I do?

PERSONAL TOUCH

Examine the following Marital Miscommunication Cycle. Mark a *2, 5,* and *10* to show where you believe your marital miscommunication fell after two, five, or ten years of marriage. (Of course if you have been married less than ten years, you will only mark the numbers that apply to the length of your marriage). If your communication has improved enough to take you off the cycle, note that as well.

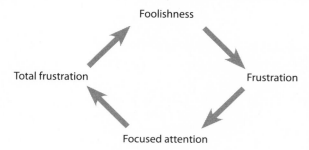

Write a one-sentence description of a memory of your conversations at the points you identified. For example,

2 years: Foolishness—I thought if I could make you understand how I felt, you would change your behavior.

5 years: Frustration—I realized you weren't going to change.

10 years: Focused attention—I learned about critical conversations and tried to practice them.

_____

_____

_____

_____

_____

After you've finished, take time to discuss your answers with your spouse.

TOUCH DOWN

Couples sometimes remain on the Marital Miscommunication Cycle because they don't understand why their conversations end in conflict. Do you need a PhD in order to communicate effectively with your mate? Not exactly. A little detective work can help you identify the core issues. Generally, these fall under definitions identified below as *PHDS*:

P *Personal Preference*: Because men and women are different and have different likes and dislikes, we approach things differently. Once you realize this, try to negotiate instead of fighting for your way. This can be an opportunity to grow as you seek to validate your spouse's desires and be supportive where you can. If the conflict pivots around your own desires, make sure you have the right motivation (James 4:3).

H *Hurts from the Past*: We all have hurts from the past that can surface in the midst of conflict. Accept this about yourself and your spouse. Look beneath the conflict, especially if the response seems more intense than the situation warrants. Ask God to reveal the underlying

Group members should have read far enough to realize they can exit this cycle of foolishness and frustration. Sometimes we learn the most from our mistakes. Ask members to identify a mistake that kept them on this Marital Miscommunication Cycle (this may come from the memory of conversations they identified in this Personal Touch). Take turns sharing lessons learned from their mistake or miscommunication.

problem or its roots. Look for possible fears triggered by the conflict: abandonment, rejection, loss of control, abuse, father wounds, and so forth.

D *Detecting Mixed-Up Miscommunication*: Miscommunications are often only misunderstandings in which no one is at fault. Instead of blaming, ask questions. Share what you heard and ask how your spouse understood things. Identify why the miscommunication took place and think through ways to avoid it. (For example, Diane and I decided to meet back at a department store entrance in an hour. We were both upset when we failed to meet up until we realized we had miscommunicated about which of the three entrances we meant.) Decide together not to focus on who is right or wrong but to work together toward healing when conflicts arise (James 3:13).

S *Sin Issues*: Sin happens in every marriage and falls within a large range of offenses: angry outbursts and loss of self-control, controlling or critical attitudes, sexual sins, emotional and physical abuse (misuse of power), name-calling or belittling, lying or deception, out-of-control spending, selfishness, and so on. True repentance and a commitment to make changes must happen in order for real healing to occur. Forgiveness can be given; trust must be earned. If the offense is ongoing, you should seek outside help from a counselor or other professional.

PERSONAL TOUCH

Write a few words to identify the most recent conflict you and your spouse had.

_____

_____

Review the definitions of PHDS and check the one that fits the underlying reason for that conflict.

☐ **P**
☐ **H**
☐ **D**
☐ **S**

Write out a new and healthier way to approach this conflict in the future. Then discuss your definitions and solutions with your spouse.

_____

_____

_____

_____

TOUCH UP

In this chapter we've examined some serious marital misunderstandings and the conflicts that result. So what's the solution? How do we begin to see our areas of blindness? In the area of intimacy, how do we move from *potential* to *experience*?

The answer may surprise you. Today's standard response goes something like this: "You need to communicate more," or, "You need to use active listening techniques." There's nothing wrong with learning to be more civil, but civility never solves the problem. It never brings you to the point of honestly seeing your blind spots and the depth of intimacy God wants to give you. Dr. John Gottman, a world-renowned expert on marital conflicts, states it clearly:

> After studying some 650 couples and tracking the fate of their marriages for up to fourteen years, we now understand that the approach of validation and active listening doesn't work, not just because it is impossible for most couples to do well, but more importantly because successful conflict resolution isn't what makes marriages succeed.[2]

I love the honesty of his research. Yet so many marriage books teach that a new communication technique will mirac-

"Paradoxically, intimacy actually comes—even grows—through conflict, disagreement, self-confrontation, and self-affirmation in Christ. These interpersonal skills allow your relationship to move toward a passionate intimacy that could not exist without the sharpening effect of conflict."
—*Sexy Christians*

Read the preceding quote aloud. Scripture teaches, "Iron sharpens iron" (Prov. 27:17). Ask, "How has God used conflict with your mate to 'sharpen' you?" Have your own answer ready and include both the source of the conflict and its positive results. Emphasize the positive. For the twelve-week plan, this marks the end of part A. Review the Home Play assignment for the next session and close in prayer.

ulously solve everything. Dr. Gottman goes on to underline the fact that when there is criticism, contempt, and defensiveness in the relationship, it is doomed.[3] When partners lack emotional self-control and discipline, the relationship will become self-destructive. We need much more than a new communication technique if we are ever going to experience in-depth intimacy. We need *critical conversations*.

What do I mean? Again, the answer may surprise you. Let's look at a passage in Scripture that is seldom used with respect to marriage although it lies at the core of the ultimate solution for our struggles with miscommunication and our hunger for deep intimacy. It presents God's solution not only for our marriages but for every area of life.

> Yes, everything else is worthless when compared with the priceless gain of knowing Christ Jesus my Lord. I have discarded everything else, counting it all as garbage, so that I may have Christ and become one with him. I no longer count on my own goodness or my ability to obey God's law, but I trust Christ to save me. For God's way of making us right with himself depends on faith. As a result, I can really know Christ and experience the mighty power that raised him from the dead. I can learn what it means to suffer with him, sharing in his death.
>
> Philippians 3:8–10 NLT

Every time I read that passage thoughtfully I find myself thinking, *Now* that's *a critical conversation*. Paul intensely describes who he is and who he longs to be. Years ago I read a fascinating study on successful people. Among these successful individuals, the research shows one predominant common factor regardless of occupation. It isn't intelligence, talent, or effort; it is *self-control*. Interestingly, the researchers found that self-control is a learned behavior with seven different components, including one central factor. That factor is *vision*—a passionate, consuming vision for life.[4]

Have you had the experience of being on the open ocean at night in a sailboat? Let's say you're attempting to return to the safety of the harbor amidst rough waves and wind.

To get back, you must do whatever is necessary to keep the harbor lights directly ahead of you. In the process, you will learn the skills necessary to keep you on course. That's a perfect picture of the power of a passionate vision.

What does that have to do with marital intimacy? Quite simply, you and your spouse are sitting together in the sailboat of life. You can take all sorts of classes and read all kinds of books on how to talk to each other in the boat. But if you haven't agreed on a destination, you can easily crash into the rocks of marital discord. Or you may experience the other popular option: drifting with the tides into an *okay* relationship.

A passionate, shared-heart vision begins with understanding yourself. *All critical conversations occur primarily within you, and sometimes they involve other people.* Reread that sentence. In other words, my life struggles are rarely about someone else; they are almost always about me.

Although I don't like that truth, it has radically changed my life and my relationship with my wife. In order to have critical conversations with those I love, I had to come out from hiding. I had to know who I am and what God has called me to do. One of the most painful experiences in life is to reach forty, fifty, or sixty years of age and not know who you are. I love to pray this prayer: *Lord, help me understand what you had in mind when you created the original* me *and enable me to become that unique and delightful person.*

PERSONAL TOUCH

It takes courage to look deeply into the mirror of our lives. When we do, we catch a glimpse of God's grace and lay the foundations for passionate communication and intimacy. Pray and take time to answer the following questions about yourself (use additional paper if needed).

1. How do you feel about who you are?

_____

_____

_____

2. How do you feel about your life?

_____

_____

_____

_____

3. How do you feel about your job?

_____

_____

_____

_____

4. What is troubling you the most right now?

_____

_____

_____

_____

After you have responded as completely as you can, share your responses with your spouse. As you listen to one another, make sure you're fully present. This exercise can become an incredible experience in critical conversations because we all long to be known and loved as we are.

TOUCH UP

You may wonder, *Wait a minute. I thought this was all about my spouse and me experiencing deep intimacy. Why do I have to spend all this time asking myself questions?* Remember: real intimacy has a surprising foundation that includes critical conversations. You were not only asking those questions of yourself. The instructions said to pray before you answered. Questions of this depth, prayerfully addressed, will eventually bring you to a point of silence before God where you listen to his answers.

Henri Nouwen eloquently expressed the connection between solitude and community:

This activity marks the start of part B for groups following the twelve-week plan. Welcome group members and open in prayer. Read the following quote aloud: "In order to have critical conversations with those I love, I had to come out from hiding. I had to know who I am and what God has called me to do." Do members agree or disagree? Prompt responses with ideas of your own but avoid dominating the group.

Why is it so important that solitude come before community?
. . . If we do not know we are the beloved sons and daughters
of God, we're going to expect someone in the community
to make us feel special and worthy. . . . But true community
is not loneliness grabbing onto loneliness.[5]

"Loneliness grabbing onto loneliness": a haunting description of the average marriage. Diane and I have coun-
seled many couples caught in the death-spiral of trying to
find their sense of worth and fulfillment in one another.
This only leads to a deepening sense of loneliness. Marriage brings us—or fails to bring us—the deepest sense of
community we will ever experience. That fulfilling sense of
community flows directly from your understanding of how
much God loves you. And underlying the critical conversations with our mate is the dialogue we have in silence before
our gracious God.

Paul cries out, "That I may know Him and the power of
His resurrection and the fellowship of His sufferings" (Phil.
3:10 NASB). The key phrase for us *eternally* is "the power
of His resurrection." The key phrase for us *emotionally* is
"the fellowship of His sufferings."

After listening to thousands of couples over more than
twenty years, I believe that becoming Sexy Christians means
facing our fears. Often, stepping into the relationship for
which God designed us—true intimacy, being uncomfortably close with the person who loves us—is our greatest
fear. We fear the openness of critical conversations because
we know they will produce pain and suffering. Here's where
you remember the goal. "The fellowship of His sufferings"
refers to suffering with a purpose. For the joy set before
him, Jesus endured the cross (Heb. 12:2). For the joy set
before you (the incredible purpose, power, and passion of
biblical intimacy), you can endure the critical—and often
uncomfortable—conversations.

PERSONAL TOUCH

Michael Dye has a great definition of what a healthy
individual's life should look like. It gives us some

clues about marital communication too. As you read his statement, circle the words that would require *critical conversations*.

no current secrets

resolving problems

identifying fears and feelings

keeping commitments to meetings, prayer, family, church, people, goals, self

being open

being honest

making eye contact

reaching out to others

increasing in relationships with God and others

accountability[6]

You should have circled almost all of the statements listed.

Ask group members to name a couple with a marriage they admire (group members excluded). Next, have them pick one or more of Dye's areas of health and explain how the couple models that quality. For example: "I know Joe and Sally make eye contact because I've seen them communicate nonverbally. They may be in the middle of a crowd, but you can tell they're connected."

TOUCH DOWN

In order to walk in health as Dye defines it, a number of critical conversations must take place. Resolving problems, identifying fears, and the other factors involve more than mere mental assent. A willingness to have critical conversations includes a commitment to pursuing biblical intimacy and the Christlike suffering it includes.

We have already mentioned that men and women are different by design. Because of these differences, men often fail to realize the power of critical conversations in the emotional (soul talk) or spiritual (spiritual talk) realms. On the other hand, women often miss the power of critical conversations in the area of physical intimacy (sex talk). When critical conversations take place in all these areas, intimacy both inside and outside the bedroom increases exponentially.

PERSONAL TOUCH

The following exercises invite you to engage in all three areas. The first exercise provides an opportunity to be honest about where you are in your physical relationship as well as where you would like to go.

Sex Talk

Check the true statements:

- ☐ Lovemaking is a good experience for my spouse.
- ☐ Lovemaking is a good experience for me.
- ☐ I enjoy the way we make love.
- ☐ Sometimes I get bored with our lovemaking.
- ☐ I would like to see more freedom or variety in our sexual activity.

Give some examples of what you mean:

_____

_____

_____

_____

_____

Check the areas you think would help enhance the quality of your sexual intimacy.

- ☐ daily passionate kissing
- ☐ planning times of intimacy
- ☐ more cuddling and nonsexual touch
- ☐ greater frequency of lovemaking (number of times per week ___)
- ☐ change in the pattern of initiating sex
- ☐ spending more time pleasuring each other's body
- ☐ making sex more fun and playful
- ☐ taking more time for lovemaking
- ☐ having erotic and exotic retreats

Express on a scale of 1 to 10 (1 low, 10 high) how much you enjoy your intimate times together. Then write down why you chose that number.

1   2   3   4   5   6   7   8   9   10
Not enjoyable   Extremely enjoyable

_____

_____

_____

_____

_____

Affirm members for their courage in these critical conversations. Ask them to rate the difficulty of Sex Talk on a scale of 1–10 (1 easy, 10 extremely difficult). Make a *Before* and *After* chart on your whiteboard or butcher paper. Ask for one-word descriptions of members' feelings *before* this critical conversation (*apprehensive, eager,* etc.) and *after* it took place (*relieved, uncertain,* etc.). Often openness and understanding are more important than the answers themselves.

After you finish, take some nonpressured time together to graciously discuss your responses. Remember, you are not trying to change your mate; you are simply sharing your world. Choose to risk the pain of critical conversations for the joy of biblical intimacy set before you.

Soul Talk

Check the answers that apply to you in your marriage right now:

- ☐ I emotionally support my spouse.
- ☐ I help create a peaceful atmosphere in our home.
- ☐ My spouse trusts me completely.
- ☐ I have my spouse's welfare in mind when making decisions.
- ☐ I am honest about how I spend money.
- ☐ When my spouse and I disagree, I don't become angry or judgmental.

Share your answers with your spouse. Look especially at the items you did not check and ask how you can change. Name one thing you could do this week that might help you move forward in an area that needs improvement.

Spiritual Talk

Name your three most negative spiritual experiences.

1. _____

2. _____

3. _____

Name your three most positive spiritual experiences.

1. _____

2. _____

3. _____

Rate your relationship with Christ (1 nonexistent, 10 extremely close).

1	2	3	4	5	6	7	8	9	10
Nonexistent									Extremely close

In which of the following ways could you grow in intimacy with Christ and others?

☐ spend more time reading his Word

☐ spend more time praying

☐ attend church regularly

☐ find new ways to serve him and others

☐ get involved in a small fellowship group

☐ make a commitment to pray together with my mate

☐ other: _____

After you complete this section, compare answers with your spouse and decide together on one thing to do this week

Sexy Christians opens with a discussion of the moment Ted and Diane met. This emphasizes the value of soul talk by highlighting the need to recall how God brought you and your spouse together. Ask each couple to share the magic of their own moment and describe how God brought them together. Emphasize that soul talk should cover both pleasant and difficult aspects of the marriage relationship.

"Every couple faces ups and downs. Feelings can diminish, especially when circumstances have led to a drifting apart. But couples who take time to mentally revisit the events that brought them together—the magic of their own unique moment—will find that although the associated feelings may lie dormant, they remain inside waiting to be revived and rediscovered."
—*Sexy Christians*

that will increase your spiritual intimacy with Christ. Write it here:

_____

_____

_____

_____

Group members who have completed all the critical conversations in this chapter have worked extremely hard. Encourage those who have not yet finished the Personal Touch exercises to do so before they move to chapter 5 material. Ask members to share:

a. the most difficult element of the critical conversations,
b. what they appreciated most about hearing their spouse's heart.

TOUCH UP

Almost two years after the incident of the miscommunication on the flight deck, Diane and I found a radical new aspect of marital unity. After the Vietnam War and a lot of prayer on my wife's part, I began connecting with God and with my wife spiritually. My most critical conversation came the day *I said yes to Christ.*

In order for you and your mate to connect as deeply as possible, I encourage you to take the same step. Scripture says, "If you confess with your mouth, 'Jesus is Lord,' and believe in your heart that God raised him from the dead, you will be saved" (Rom. 10:9). So if you've never done so, you may pray this simple prayer and know God will honor it:

Dear God, I realize I can never have the marriage you intended without Jesus as Savior and Lord in my life. I ask your forgiveness for the wrong things I have done. Please come into my life right now. I want to follow you wholeheartedly. I want you to be Lord over my marriage. Thank you for hearing my prayer and coming into my life. Amen.

As you continue with the critical conversations in your marriage, I encourage you to pray. When you tried to talk about these things in the past, your temper may have flared as mine did. When that happens, communication ends. But Diane and I are living proof that God can do some miraculous things in your life if you are willing to trust him, make an effort to move into your spouse's world, and listen with all your heart.

Note: As you completed the exercises in this chapter, you may have felt stuck regarding certain issues. Perhaps you had heated or irresolvable discussions. Just as the plane captain interrupted Diane's potentially deadly decision, sometimes we need outside help from professionals who can help us interrupt potentially deadly patterns in our marriages. If you need help resolving issues or feel stuck as a couple, seek outside help from your pastor or a Christian counselor. They can often help you maneuver your way successfully through any bumps you encounter as you prepare to soar together.

5

Honesty

Ultimate Challenge to Biblical Intimacy

TED

IN TOUCH

Sometimes we walk through life hiding things. We hide so we can live without having to be accountable. Why? We're scared. We don't want to be embarrassed, hurt, or looked down on.

For many years, that was my story. I always thought if I could keep my secret life hidden, I would overcome. I did okay for a while; at least I thought I was okay. In reality, I couldn't function. I was rooted in a hidden and deeply addictive lifestyle. I knew I was going down, and I did. I hit rock bottom.

I only found healing after I began to get honest with myself, my family, my friends, and especially God. Proverbs 21:3 (NLT) says, "The LORD is . . . pleased when we do what is right and just."

come clean with yourself, your mate, and your God.

He never says it will be easy, though. In our *Pure Desire Men's* group, we have a saying: "Doing the right thing is the hard thing." For me, honesty was difficult. I had to learn to be vulnerable and transparent as I made myself accountable. The phone calls and weekly meetings helped me see that honesty enables the Holy Spirit to work.

I reached a time of crossroads. I could deny what had happened or be honest and let God take it from there. I chose God. I already knew him, but I had my own agenda. My poor choices had hurt many people. For years I had chosen my addiction over family, friends, and God. It took time—a long time—to regain the trust of those (including myself) who had heard my lies. One of my friends told me I had to become "brutally honest." I finally got it. In my first men's accountability group I let it all out. For the first time, I felt the enemy back away. I shared things most people would never discuss. My decision to become brutally honest changed my life.

The toughest part is looking back on the hurt I caused my family. I never thought my secret life would get out and we would endure so much pain. But God took that pain and used it. He began working differently in each of us, and it began with my honesty.

When I truly made the commitment to be honest, God turned what the enemy meant for evil into the most important piece in my life. Today I love to share my story. My honesty lets others know it is okay to share, and that gives them hope.

Honesty hurts. But God will always be there, and he "delights in those who tell the truth" (Prov. 12:22 NLT).—*Rob*

Open in prayer and ask members to review the following quote and their Personal Touch graphs. Ask them to share how and why (or why not) they have found the statement to be true in their own lives. Be ready to give an example to get things started.

"Why do we find it so hard to have an honest conversation with God? The answer to that question is critical because the depth of intimacy we have with our partner directly reflects our intimacy with God."
—*Sexy Christians*

PERSONAL TOUCH

The close tie between intimacy with God and intimacy with your mate is a central feature of the Sexy Christians message. How has that worked in your life? On the graph below, trace a line to show your closeness to God at various times. Trace a line directly over the main line (God) to represent times when you were extremely close to him; move your line farther away for times when you were not as close. An example is shown below.

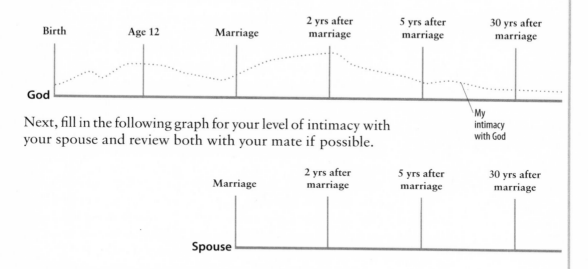

Next, fill in the following graph for your level of intimacy with your spouse and review both with your mate if possible.

TOUCH DOWN

We pulled into the chapel parking lot and smiled at the scrubbed clean look common to all military bases. A class of officer candidates ran past, and I remembered women could now enter the program. The muscular Marine drill instructor shouting orders alongside made no comments about "running them into the ground." A lot had changed in thirty years.

While in the area on business, Diane and I had decided to return to the Pensacola Naval Air Station and the chapel where we were married. As we stood in the tiny chapel, all the excitement and anxiety of our wedding day returned: sheer joy combined with a deep fear of the unknown. In many ways, ours was the typical wedding. I couldn't even repeat my vows correctly! Since that time, I've performed hundreds of wedding ceremonies and observed that same joy and bewilderment in the eyes of countless young couples.

On our wedding day, Diane and I exploded out of the chapel, charged underneath the traditional archway of swords, and ran down the steps into an uncertain future. Standing on those same steps so many years later, I was stunned by the great things God had done in our lives. I also remembered the painful struggles and problems we faced along the way.

Even in the earliest days of our marriage, something in our hearts irresistibly pulled us forward. Remember the wonderful scene in J. R. R. Tolkien's *Lord of the Rings* series? Tolkien beautifully describes the incident in which it becomes clear someone must return the Ring to the land of Mordor and face Sauron's evil attacks. No one rushes to take the job. Finally, tentatively, Frodo Baggins steps forward and utters the classic line, "I will take the Ring, though I do not know the way."

Significant life changes require courage because we rarely know the way. Marriage is a journey rather than a destination, so it leads us to make other decisions that require courage. In fact, our marital journey leads to a whole series of challenges and efforts we never planned to face.

In one of the great lines of popular psychological literature, Scott Peck writes that mental health is a "commitment to reality at all costs."[1] Real intimacy—Sexy Christians style—is only possible when both partners are mentally healthy because it involves becoming uncomfortably close to another imperfect human being. Unless you are healthy, intimacy will seriously mess with your mind. And what's the final, critical element of true intimacy? *Honesty*.

T—Trust, O—Openness, U—Understanding, C—Critical Conversations, H—Honesty.

We've already asked many questions that have challenged us to be honest about ourselves. The greatest challenge, however, is being honest about who we are in God's sight. I've always found this a difficult concept to grasp. Yet Scripture declares that I am:

- victorious in Christ (Rev. 21:7).
- complete in Christ (Col. 2:10).
- beloved of God (Rom. 1:7; Col. 3:12; 1 Thess. 1:4).

Every day I review more than fifty verses during my morning devotional time to remind myself of how God the Father sees me in Christ. If I don't read them daily, the voices in my head from the past and the mistakes I make in the present combine to confuse me. With the help of my wife, I'm usually honest about how far and how often I fall short. Yet I must also be honest about how God sees me in Christ.

PERSONAL TOUCH

About which of the following statements from the Word of God do you need to be honest? God proclaims it: *this is the truth about you.* Do you honestly believe them? Place a star beside those you need to embrace more completely:

☐ I am forgiven of all my sins and washed in the blood (Eph. 1:7; Heb. 9:14).

☐ I am a temple where the Holy Spirit lives (1 Cor. 6:19).

☐ I am set free (John 8:31–33).

☐ I am dead to sin (Rom. 6:2).

☐ I am accepted in Jesus Christ (Eph. 1:6).

☐ I am free from condemnation (Rom. 8:1).

☐ I am called of God (2 Tim. 1:9).

☐ I have the mind of Christ (Phil. 2:5).

☐ I have the peace of God, which transcends all understanding (Phil. 4:7).

☐ I can do all things in and through Christ Jesus (Phil. 4:13).

Of the statements you marked, which has the potential to have the most impact on your marriage?

_____

_____

_____

_____

Why do you think this is true?

_____

_____

_____

Encourage couples to turn their chairs to face each other and hold hands. Those without spouses present can pair up or borrow a leader. Model this by sitting as directed and telling your spouse, "(*Name*), you are forgiven of your sins." The response will be "I, (*Name*), am forgiven of my sins." Have your spouse repeat the statement to you using your name. Repeat one final time using your own name. Follow this pattern for the entire list. Afterward discuss the experience.

"God's love is literally beyond our ability to comprehend. You never have to fear that God doesn't want you or will reject you. He can't do it because he loves you outrageously, amazingly, and eternally."
—*Sexy Christians*

What changes might you see if you embraced its truth?

_____

_____

_____

TOUCH DOWN

Another challenge to marital honesty arises from the tendency we all have to wear masks. Because we don't truly believe what God says about us, we wear masks designed to keep others from knowing the truth about who we are and what we do.

Like the Wizard of Oz, we push the buttons and pull the levers as fast as we can until God allows Toto to reveal everything. In fact, I like to call marriage the ultimate *Toto experience*. No matter how often we cry, "Don't look behind the curtain," our family still catches glimpses of the truth.

We wear masks because they work. Today, most of us keep busy with email, voice mail, instant mail, and snail mail. We don't have time to remove our masks, so when folks ask how we're doing, we respond, "Fine." If we took time to share the truth, no one would have time to listen to everything we said anyway.

Our pop-driven culture sometimes looks more like a masquerade ball than reality. And the masquerade-ball beliefs about marriage are nothing but crazy! I came home early one day and accidentally flipped on *Oprah* instead of the news. A popular Hollywood starlet was dispensing advice about how to catch and keep a man. This woman had been married so many times she had rice marks on her face! And this is the one we choose to tell us how to have a meaningful relationship?

If you follow the starlet-style marital advice, you will definitely wear a mask. When you follow the pop beliefs of our culture and they don't work, you end up sure there's something wrong with you. You have to hide your obvious incompetence, so you put on a mask.

PERSONAL TOUCH

What masks have you worn? Use the chart below to list them, past and present. In the first column list all the masks you have worn during your life, dividing them into the three types—funny, painful, denial. Then use the second column to list which of those masks you have worn in your marriage.

Looking at Our Masks

Masks I have worn throughout my life	Masks (past and present) I have worn in my marriage
Funny Masks:	
Painful Masks:	
Denial Masks:	

What were the benefits of wearing these masks? For example: "a clown mask deflected criticism from my classmates and helped hide the shame of my mom's mental illness." Discuss the masks and their benefits with your spouse.

We can all think of times we've worn masks. This exercise should have revealed unknown masks and brought new honesty into marriages. Sometimes we use masks to help survive difficult situations. Ask group members to give an example from their lives such as: "A mask of apathy helped me survive my stepdad's constant criticism." Next ask them to reexamine the lists they completed in this Personal Touch. Which masks do they use in times of stress? Which masks do they most want to throw away and why?

TOUCH DOWN

An additional challenge arises because of our need to be honest about God's call on our lives. We all carry an incredible, unfathomable call placed on us by God himself. No, this doesn't mean everyone must become a priest or pastor. Before the beginning of time, God designed you as a unique human being and you and your mate as a unique couple (1 Peter 2:9). You have a distinctive call that's beyond your ability to accomplish. It stretches far beyond you as an individual and as a couple. Yet God specifically gave it to you because of your *inability* to accomplish it. It will require your best, but he alone can bring it to pass.

Why would Frodo's challenge to return the Ring be an appropriate marriage analogy? Many married people live as though they carry two opposing rings. The first is the signet ring from their family of origin. The second is the wedding ring from their spouse. For some individuals, the family of origin ring that marks their heritage matches beautifully with the wedding ring that denotes their future. For others, the signet ring of family both defines and traps them in patterns of the past. It sabotages their dreams and confronts them with the same challenge Frodo accepted. In the introduction, we pointed out that in this workbook we would:

Revisit the wounds of the past through the gift of marriage.
Refine our hearts through the strength God gives.
Respond together to our calling in Christ.

Do you understand that marriage is part of a larger process? When you ran down the aisle on your wedding day, God had already placed promises, dreams, and hopes in your heart. He works to help you understand those promises and that calling throughout your life together. Of course you may not have seen your dreams for your marriage as promises from God. Some may have arisen from your own romantic fantasies. But I have performed enough weddings to realize that God places his promises in the hearts of every couple who walks down the aisle in love with each other and with him. The conflicts of the days ahead—the conflicts of the rings—will force them to *revisit* the wounds of the past. And the promises God has placed within them will challenge them to *refine* their hearts as they cry out for God's best in their marriage. Only then will they be able to *respond* together to his call.

PERSONAL TOUCH

What are some personal promises God has given you for the years ahead? List them below along with the way you feel about each one.

Promise	How I feel about it

What are the promises God has given you for your marriage, for your children, for your family? How do you feel about each one?

Promise	How I feel about it

Make a chart on your whiteboard or butcher paper similar to the one here but labeled, *God's Promise* and *How I Feel about It*. Give an example of a promise such as, "I will never leave you nor forsake you" (Heb. 13:5 NKJV) and a corresponding feeling such as, "Uncertain because my father deserted our family." List and discuss two or three others.

This marks the end of part A for the twelve-week plan. Review next week's Home Play assignment and dismiss in prayer.

If possible, take a few minutes to share your answers with your spouse. Be especially open to each other's feelings. As you listen carefully, you will gain some special insights into your partner's heart and God-given calling as well as your calling together.

TOUCH UP

I've assigned this exercise often over the past thirty years. It is amazing how these simple questions can open a person's heart. Many couples have never considered God's promises for them. Folks who have been walking with Christ for a while seem to share a common question about his promises: *Why do they take so long?*

We confront a unique paradox when it comes to the promises God speaks into our lives. He is always more interested in the *process* of the promise than its completion or fulfillment. In the process, we realize who we are. In the process, we discover his outrageous love. In the process, his grace strengthens our hearts. In the process, our marriage becomes what we had hoped for all along. And in the process, God brings us to an intimacy—with him and with one another—that we never thought possible.

We can see this process throughout Scripture. Let's start with Joseph in the Old Testament. His life begins to change with the coming of a God-given dream that all of his brothers will bow down before him. This snot-nosed kid loudly proclaims to anyone nearby that before long, his brothers will be his servants.

In his hyperdysfunctional home, Joseph's words are a red flag to a raging bull. He experiences the first element of the process: *the call.* God is showing him his purpose and destiny. And his response is similar to the responses I've seen in others who hear a promise from God about a transition. They seem to assume things will move ahead rapidly. Often they miss a key truth: *Our striving never fulfills God's promises.* We don't have to work and push to make them happen. They happen naturally once our character matches the promise.

As our character grows, the promise will flow into completion as part of a natural-supernatural process. Examine what David says about *process* in Joseph's life:

> He sent a man ahead of them. He sent Joseph, who was sold as a slave. They hurt his feet with shackles, and cut into his neck with an iron collar. The LORD's promise tested him through fiery trials until his prediction came true. The king sent someone to release him. The ruler of nations set him free. He made Joseph the master of his palace and the ruler of all his possessions.
>
> Psalm 105:17–21 GW

David describes the experience of receiving an incredible promise from God about his destiny. Imagine receiving such a promise. Its wonder overwhelms us. But suddenly, it seems as though God has pushed us into a fistfight in a dark room. We receive the promise and its exact opposite occurs. The honeymoon has ended, and we disagree about nearly everything. Welcome to the process.

God sends Ananias to the apostle-to-be Paul to speak God's promise over him. He foretells Paul's incredible future: he will stand before kings and nations. In the same breath he reveals that Paul will suffer much for the cause of Christ (Acts 9:15–16). Welcome to the process.

PERSONAL TOUCH

Take time to examine some other biblical figures who experienced the process of the promise. Review the Scriptures that accompany each name and complete the remainder of the chart as shown in the example.

If you're following the twelve-week plan, this section marks the start of part B. Review for the group the Touch Up Bible teaching given here. If time allows, share (or have a group member share) about a time when God took you through a process before he fulfilled his promise.

"Most of us want to grow up, but few want the struggle of the growth process. I'm convinced God created marriage to build in us a hunger for real inner growth despite the pain it yields."—*Sexy Christians*

Biblical figure	God's promise	Crisis or problem	Fulfillment
Abram Genesis 12; 15–18	*Your descendants will outnumber the stars.*	*He and Sarai were old; she was barren.*	*Birth of Isaac and the nation of Israel.*
Moses Exodus 6:1–3; 7:1–12:42; 14:1–31			
Joshua Joshua 1:1–20:9; 21:43–45			
Reader's choice			

Duplicate some or all of this chart on whiteboard or butcher paper. Ask group members to share their ideas for one of the biblical figures. Next, have members share their answers for the fourth column. Make sure to clarify the crisis (process) along with the final fulfillment.

TOUCHDOWN

The promises God speaks into your life about you and your marriage will test you. But there's good news: you can never fail a test God gives; you simply retake it until you pass. At times marriage can seem like one long remedial test. God gives a promise about your marriage. With that promise still fresh in your mind, you experience the opposite reality. You can so easily fail the test by tossing a cutting remark toward your spouse. Yet notice God's kindness. Anyone else would write you off, stamp *failure* on your forehead, and call you a loser. Your spouse may be tempted to do that at times, but God never does.

The amazing thing about the ways of God in our lives and marriages is that *testing becomes the foundation of who we are*. Testing became the making of Joseph and Paul. Testing establishes us in the things God wants to give us. He will not give us the promises on our terms. He is God and we are not. Testing drives the truth of that statement into our lives.

The divine contradiction: we don't reach God's promise by going up but by going *down*. God always takes us to the pit before the pinnacle. He took Joseph to prison and Paul to persecution. But do you recognize the best part? *He promises to go with us everywhere we go.*

Diane and I are opposites in so many ways. I view a trip to the airport as an adventure. I usually don't look at the flight schedule until I'm on my way. I love to discover what lies ahead as I experience it. That's why I sometimes forget my passport or a piece of luggage. I never see this as a problem; it just makes the trip more exciting. But when Diane accompanied me, these careless habits led to some huge arguments at the ticket counter. This could get rather embarrassing because many of the folks from the church we pastored worked at the airport.

God had given me a promise that Diane and I would minister together more and experience a new season of intimacy. As the arguments escalated, I told God he must have made a mistake because Diane was too controlling. Finally, honesty entered the picture and I looked around the pit I had dug. Of course, Jesus was there all along. He showed me how important safety was to Diane. My family-of-origin ring was a lifestyle of risk. I escaped the pain of my upbringing by living on adrenaline. Finally, I threw off the old ring and exchanged it for the ring of promise. I bent my knee to my wife's needs. I asked her, "How can I make you feel safe on the next trip?" One simple request changed everything. I went down, and suddenly we were soaring together.

At times, God may take you in the opposite direction from his promise so he can bring you to a place just for the two of you. In *Sexy Christians* I pointed out that every marriage eventually runs into a stalemate where you disagree about reality. You argue about who's right or wrong. Your mate is not affirming you, and you feel alone. Here you experience your deepest contradictions. But here in the stalemate, you mine out the treasures of your faith.

As you face the crisis, you have two options: get bitter or discover that your relationship with God means more to you than anyone or anything. In such moments, something happens deep in your soul. Simply put, *you get better*. You get better at life, better at loving, better at being yourself in God's presence. Some of the things you learn in the tension of contradiction and crisis will be with you for the rest of your life. You find joy in the process of moving from hope to manifestation, from promise to fulfillment.

So many avoid the process because they know growth involves pain. We all know someone who has a problem everyone around can see clearly. The individual with the problem can—and does—describe it in detail, explaining what the problem is in the marriage or relationship and describing exactly how to fix it. Yet no action ever takes place. And the worst case scenario occurs when that person is *you*.

As I observe folks in the counseling office, I've seen it often. Lack of action is one of the most significant obstacles to growth. It's repeatedly choosing to pay later instead of paying now. When you don't get honest and face the choices you need to make, you incur a high interest rate and penalties too. That makes honesty one of the most important skills you need to build a great marriage.

PERSONAL TOUCH

As you pursue honesty in your marriage, you can't overlook what I call life's *quiet crossroads*. They're *quiet* because we can choose to ignore them if we wish. But character rises from the decisions we make—whether anyone is looking or not—that directs our paths toward openness and understanding.

What are your quiet crossroads? What decision do you need to make? Honesty confronts us with the need for change, and real change involves a specific plan with sequential steps. What decision have you put off? Examine one or more by answering the following questions. Recognize that this chart can apply to your physical health, career, spiritual life, and of course marriage.

Crossroads decision	Steps I must take	What will happen in my life	Difficulty level (1 easy, 10 difficult)	Importance (1 important, 10 unimportant)
Example: *Become financially solvent*	a. *Cut up credit cards* b. *Pay off all debt other than house payment*	a. *Greater financial security* b. *Greater peace and discipline*	*9*	*1*

TOUCH UP

Betrayal can keep us stuck in life and unable to deal with the quiet crossroads. The people who should have been Joseph's strongest supporters betrayed him instead. Paul's own Jewish brothers stoned him to death. I think it essential that at some point in life we become wounded. Paul expressed it vividly when he prayed we would "know the fel-

One of this group's strengths is mutual prayer. Briefly review the previous Touch Down about testing. If your group is large, divide into smaller groups to discuss individual answers. Then ask the couples in each group to pray for each other.

lowship of [Christ's] sufferings" (Phil. 3:10 NASB). As we discussed in the previous chapter, suffering with a purpose is the gateway to knowing resurrection power.

When you understand that betrayal and woundedness are part of normal spiritual development, you forgive more easily. God doesn't cause the pain in our lives. Instead, he uses it to refine our hearts. Joseph felt deeply wounded by his brothers' betrayal. Scripture tells us he begged for help but they wouldn't listen (Gen. 42:21). And Paul frequently despaired for his life because of the repeated betrayals he experienced. But both men discovered an amazing truth: *when your life goes in the opposite direction from your calling, your calling returns to the hands of God.* And God never lets it slip from his grasp. He simply dusts your fingerprints off and hands it back to you. In the process, you learn to trust him at a deeper level.

At this point of crisis, the Holy Spirit brings us to the place where we can learn to trust God with everything without worry, fear, or depression. Next, the Holy Spirit does an even deeper refining work: he brings us to the place where *God can trust us.* Of course God always loves us, but he bases his trust on our character.

I no longer resent the wounds I receive. Since they're inevitable, building walls to protect myself is a waste of time. Instead I allow God to heal me. What flows *from* me is far more important than what happens *against* me. I refuse to live with a suspicious, cynical, distrustful heart. So many folks make comments like, "I trust God, but I don't trust anyone else." In truth, they don't trust God either. The walls they've built against others keep him at a distance as well.

Joseph faces the process of the promise more than once. He goes from the pit to Potiphar's house, where he is betrayed again. He ends up in Pharaoh's prison, where he is betrayed once more. God's process can contain many cycles, but his whole goal is to bring us to the final stage: *clarity.*

In Genesis 45 Joseph makes one of the greatest confessions in the Old Testament. When they finally recognize Joseph and realize his incredible authority in Pharaoh's kingdom, his brothers bow before him. In his moment of clarity, he places no blame. Marvelously, he understands God was at work to orchestrate his sovereign purposes despite the pain. Joseph understands that his brothers are simply instruments God used to change him. That doesn't excuse their behavior, but it does make sense of the outcome.

This also explains why vindication is a waste of time. It is foolish to wait for God to vindicate us for past wounds. Sometimes God turns up the heat on your marriage, pulls you out of the oven, and sticks a fork in you. If you're not tender enough, he returns you to the broiling pan. After all, his long-term goal is not your vindication but your maturation.

Joseph goes through this cycle of up and down at least three distinct times. Paul's entire life is a series of these cycles. When you have climbed up one mountain and experienced an incredible high in marriage, you can't just jump to the next peak. You have to go down the mountain because you have to unlearn some things as you travel. If you believe God has called you to have a great marriage and you only have a good one, you will have to go down low in order to rise up. If you don't allow God to take you to the depths, he can't take you to the heights.

These truths are impossible to live without a clear sense of direction. Joseph has a clear dream from God. Paul has a clear promise spoken over him by Ananias. Most of us don't have such dramatically vivid times of guidance. Instead, the Holy Spirit speaks subtly and deeply to us as we take time from our insane pace to pull over to the side of the road. There we can have moments of meditation during which we think about the gift we'll leave behind.

FINISHING TOUCH

What gift has God called you to give to those who follow you? What gift has he called your marriage to give to your world? Over the next week, take some time to think about what gift God wants you to leave behind. (See the chart below.)

If you're struggling, let the Holy Spirit enable you to dream again. If you're caught up in the frenetic blur of day-to-day survival, slow down, raise your head and heart to heaven, and allow God to give you a new perspective. God designed your life and your marriage to make a difference. Let Christ convince you of this fact afresh.

Next, take some time apart as a couple. Your life together is more than just paying off a mortgage, raising the kids, and graduating to a hole in the ground. God's hand brought you together to give a divine gift to this world. What are your finest achievements, greatest experiences, and best relationships? What are your life goals together? What are the character issues in your marriage that still need development? What will be said about you two after you finish this race of life? Will it be, "They really loved each other," "They cared and reached out to those in need," "They had great kids," "They deeply loved God." Share your thoughts with one another as you complete the chart.

The Gift God Wants Me to Leave Behind—Past and Present

Achievements to date	Great experiences	Real relationships
1.	1.	1.
2.	2.	2.
3.	3.	3.
4.	4.	4.

The Gift God Wants Me to Leave Behind—Future

Achievements to accomplish	Experiences to have	Relationships to develop
1.	1.	1.
2.	2.	2.
3.	3.	3.
4.	4.	4.

The Gift God Wants Me to Leave Behind—Future and Legacy

Life goals and character development in the years ahead	What will be said of me in the end?
1.	1.
2.	2.
3.	3.
4.	4.
5.	5.

 Take time to review this Finishing Touch. Give each couple a piece of butcher paper and markers or crayons. Have them draw a picture of one goal they hope to achieve, one dream they hope to realize, or one way they hope to be remembered together. Then ask the couples to share their picture and its meaning. Review the location of the Personal Touch assignment for the final session (appendix 3), and close in prayer.

 "None of us has to settle for mere side-by-side existence, stuck in the foothills of a stalemate or frustration. We can live on the fiery mountain of intimacy. We can get uncomfortably close and vulnerable. We can open up and share truthfully, even at the risk of deep pain. Yes, we'll face fire and pain, but we're willing to pay the price because we've caught a glimpse of the mountaintop and the wonders it holds."
—*Sexy Christians*

Appendix 1

Small Group Leaders' Tips

We offer the following suggestions to help you guide others through the *Sexy Christians Workbook*.

Equipment and Supplies: For each session you will need to provide seating room for everyone, pens or pencils, and a whiteboard or supply of butcher paper and markers to record group responses or provide information. You may also want to have a few extra Bibles and a blank copy or two of the workbook available. The Leader Lines will highlight any special supplies for individual sessions.

Preparation: All group members should do their best to prepare in advance during the week by working through the lessons in the workbook and optional accompanying chapters in *Sexy Christians*. As the leader, you will want to make sure you complete both of these preparatory steps. Next, familiarize yourself with the Quick Quotes and Leader Lines in the margins of the workbook for each session. Mark the Leader Lines you especially want to cover and add any additional notes or adaptations specific to your group. In addition, visit the Sexy Christians website to find the extra leader downloads we've posted (www.sexychristians.com).

Group Format and Dynamics: Your openness and understanding as you lead the group is as important as your personal preparation since it sets the tone for the group interaction. We've designed the sessions to move from less invasive commentary to more probing questions and exercises. Emphasizing the importance of preparation will help each group session flow smoothly.

Study your group carefully and gauge your questions and discussion points accordingly. Your goal as a leader is to encourage and support each member without causing unnecessary pain or embarrassment. Don't be afraid to intervene if you see the discussion moving in a potentially harmful direction. This requires a delicate balance, so take time daily to pray for your group members and the study. If you encounter an especially difficult situation, seek help from your pastor or other church leader. And don't forget to contact us at www.sexychristians.com. We'll be glad to assist you in any way possible.

Confidentiality: Group members must understand and commit to the truth that *information shared in the group setting must remain there*. Although the Sexy Christians truths can and should extend beyond the small group setting, personal information about individuals or couples should not. Please emphasize this important truth with group members and consider praying a prayer of commitment or covenant that includes this important aspect of your group relationship.

Adaptability: This essential quality allows you to go with the flow of your group and especially with the leading of the Holy Spirit. Prepare in advance, but allow God to guide you as you move through the material. If your group lingers on a question that addresses a genuine need, don't rush ahead. Feel free to spend more time on less material rather than rush through for the mere sake of completion.

Schedules vary, so we offer two plans for completing this workbook. The first (appendix 4) is a six- or seven-week session. The other (appendix 5; our preferred option) covers twelve weeks or a full quarter of study. Or make up your own plan and adapt as needed.

Appendix 2

Introductory Session

In Sexy Christians material, no one has homework, but everyone has Home Play. The Home Play assignment for this initial session (used in either study plan) asks members to complete only two Personal Touch exercises ahead of time (see pp. 127 and 129). Instruct those who do not have workbooks to visit www.sexychristians.com to find the assignment (or print it from the site yourself and pass out copies when couples register for the class).

From this session forward, we ask you to do your best to ensure every participant has a workbook. We suggest you have workbooks and the book *Sexy Christians* available at this introductory session.

As the leader, you will also need to prepare by reading the introduction and T.O.U.C.H. Points sections before this session. Take time to extend personal invitations and to pray for those who will join your group.

Open the session with a brief prayer. Welcome participants and acknowledge the sacrifices they've made in order to attend. Introduce yourself and your spouse by telling briefly how you met. You should each tell a portion of the story if possible.

Next, go around the group and ask other members to introduce themselves and share the story of how they met. You may share the connection between these stories and the first chapter in *Sexy Christians* (suggested reading to supplement this course). Refer to the schedule in appendix 4 or 5 for a suggested meeting schedule. You may also download the form at www.sexychristians.com ("Workbook Downloads"), add your own study dates, and photocopy it for group members.

Use the following question, adapted from a Home Play assignment in *Sexy Christians*, to help members begin to feel comfortable in the group setting. Ask members to respond aloud. Next, pass around copies of *Sexy Christians*. Briefly go through the T.O.U.C.H. Points and study procedure. If possible, distribute a schedule that lists the chapters, topics, and assignments to be covered matched with appropriate chapters from *Sexy Christians* (see appendix 4 or 5 for an adaptable schedule).

PERSONAL TOUCH

If you're part of a group studying this workbook together, please complete this initial (and fun) assignment before your first meeting. If you're studying alone or with your spouse, this will be your first assignment too.

Which answer best describes the first thing that came to mind when you saw the title of this workbook?

    a. What on earth is a "Sexy Christian"?
    b. Oh no, another book about wrapping yourself in plastic wrap or painting each other's toenails.
    c. What a great idea!
    d. I don't know what that is, but it definitely sounds interesting.

Examine the following list of internal attributes. Some of these qualities drew you together when you and your mate first met. Go through the list twice. First, write an *I* beside the attributes that *initially* attracted you to your mate. Next, go through the list again and write a *D* beside the attributes you have since *discovered* about your spouse. Let's begin your adventure together.

____ Adventurous	____ Good listener	____ Positive
____ Artistic	____ Good provider	____ Problem solver
____ Athletic	____ Good sense of humor	____ Reliable
____ Authentic	____ Good sense of self-esteem	____ Responsible
____ Caring	____ Good work ethic	____ Romantic
____ Committed to Christ	____ Honest	____ Self-controlled
____ Compassionate	____ Hospitable	____ Sincere
____ Confident	____ Humble	____ Stable
____ Considerate	____ Intelligent	____ Sympathetic
____ Courageous	____ Joyful	____ Teachable
____ Creative	____ Kind	____ Thoughtful
____ Dependable	____ Leadership qualities	____ Transparent
____ Disciplined	____ Loving	____ Trusting
____ Enthusiastic	____ Loyal	____ Trustworthy
____ Faithful	____ Optimistic	____ Understanding
____ Fun-loving	____ Organized	____ Values relationships
____ Generous	____ Outgoing	____ Vulnerable
____ Gentle	____ Passionate	____ Other:
____ Genuine	____ Patient	____ Other:
____ Giving	____ Peaceful	____ Other:

Take time to discuss both lists with your spouse. The apostle Paul gives some great advice about relationships when he writes, "I'd say you will do best by filling your minds and meditating on things true, noble, reputable, authentic, compelling, gracious—the best, not the worst; the beautiful, not the ugly; things to praise, not things to curse" (Phil. 4:8 *Message*). Give thanks to God for the positive attributes he has given you through the wonderful gift of your mate.

"Your spouse is a gift from God. You didn't meet by accident. If you have said yes to Christ, you serve an omniscient and awesome God. He was at work in your life long before you were conscious of his touch."
—*Sexy Christians*

LEADER LINES

As you point group members to the preceding Personal Touch exercise, take a moment to discuss the truth of the accompanying quote (not the details of their answers). God was already at work to draw husbands and wives together regardless of whether they recognized it when they met. If appropriate, share ways you saw evidence of God's work in your initial meeting with your spouse. Others may add to the discussion if time allows. If group dynamics allow, ask each couple to share a prayer need or goal for the study and pray for these needs as you close. Before the session, prepare your own request so you can share it first.

Appendix 3

Sexy Christians Celebration

You've spent several weeks doing the hard work of building intimacy into your life and your marriage. It's time to celebrate! You and your spouse should complete the following exercise together if possible.

Near the end of chapter 5, you explored the gifts you hope to leave behind. As you conclude this study, work together to construct a collage that shows the legacy your marriage will give to others. Use clippings, magazine artwork, wedding or other photographs, and anything else you choose that expresses God's work in your marriage. Design this together to express your heart for one another, our hurting world, and our Lord. Choose the contents intentionally and be ready to share the meaning behind your collage with the other members of your group.

LEADER LINES

Your group members have come a long way in a short time. Celebrate God's work through them and through the *Sexy Christians Workbook* in this concluding session. Since this is an informal time, you may want to consider sharing a meal together. Open in a brief prayer and ask group members to share about a Personal Touch, Touch Up, or other portion of the study they found particularly meaningful and why. If possible, allow all members to contribute to the discussion. Keep the tone positive and emphasize God's good work in the lives of group members.

Next, ask them to share the collages they made in the preceding Personal Touch. Each couple should display their collage and explain why they chose the items they did. Members who did not complete a collage should tell the group about some of the legacies their marriage will leave.

Share in a time of affirmation by speaking words of encouragement over each couple. Tell them the good things you see in their marriage and affirm them concerning God's plans to take them further into biblical intimacy. Close in prayer for the group and for the individual marriages, thanking God for his work in the lives of these Sexy Christians.

Appendix 4

Six- or Seven-Week Group Study Plan

*H*ome Play Assignments: In Sexy Christians material, no one has homework, but everyone has *Home Play*. The Home Play for each chapter or portion of a chapter consists of completing the workbook reading for that week and any Personal Touch exercises it contains. If possible, go over your answers with your spouse before the group session. Recommended reading in *Sexy Christians* is suggested but not required.

Week 1: Introductory Session   Meeting Date:

_____

Home Play Assignment: Before this session, complete the two Personal Touch exercises found in appendix 2.

Week 2: Trust   Meeting Date:

_____

Home Play Assignment: Before this session, read the Introduction, T.O.U.C.H. Points, and chapter 1, Trust. Complete all Personal Touch exercises.

Recommended Reading: Introduction and chapters 1–2 of *Sexy Christians*.

Week 3: Openness   Meeting Date:

_____

Home Play Assignment: Before this week's session, read chapter 2, Openness, and complete all Personal Touch exercises.

Recommended Reading: Chapters 3–5 of *Sexy Christians*.

Week 4: Understanding   Meeting Date:

_____

Home Play Assignment: Before this week's session, read chapter 3, Understanding, and complete all Personal Touch exercises.

Recommended Reading: Chapters 6–8 of *Sexy Christians*.

Week 5: Critical Conversations   Meeting Date:

_____

Home Play Assignment: Before this week's session, read chapter 4, Critical Conversations, and complete all Personal Touch exercises.

Recommended Reading: Chapters 9–10 of *Sexy Christians*.

Week 6: Honesty   Meeting Date:

_____

Home Play Assignment: Before this week's session, read chapter 5, Honesty, and complete all Personal Touch exercises.

Recommended Reading: Chapters 11–12 of *Sexy Christians*.

Week 7 (Optional): Sexy Christians Celebration
Meeting Date: _____

Home Play Assignment: Before this week's session, complete the Personal Touch exercise found in appendix 3.

Appendix 5

Twelve-Week Group Study Plan

*H*ome Play Assignments: In Sexy Christians material, no one has homework, but everyone has *Home Play*. The Home Play for each chapter or portion of a chapter consists of completing the workbook reading for that week and any Personal Touch exercises it contains. If possible, go over your answers with your spouse before the group session. Recommended reading in *Sexy Christians* is suggested but not required.

Week 1: Introductory Session   Meeting Date: _____

(see Leader Lines for a plan for this session)

Week 2: Trust, Part A   Meeting Date: _____

Home Play Assignment: Before this session, read the introduction, T.O.U.C.H. Points, and chapter 1, Trust, from the beginning of the chapter through Personal Touch on page 24.

Recommended Reading: Introduction and chapter 1 of *Sexy Christians*.

Week 3: Trust, Part B   Meeting Date:

_____

Home Play Assignment: Before this session, read the rest of chapter 1, Trust, from Touchdown on page 24 through the end of the chapter.

Recommended Reading: Chapter 2 of *Sexy Christians*.

Week 4: Openness, Part A   Meeting Date:

_____

Home Play Assignment: Before this session, read chapter 2, Openness, from the beginning of the chapter through Personal Touch on page 47.

Recommended Reading: Chapters 3–4 of *Sexy Christians*.

Week 5: Openness, Part B   Meeting Date:

_____

Home Play Assignment: Before this session, read the rest of chapter 2, Openness, from Touch Up at the bottom of page 47 through the end of the chapter.

Recommended Reading: Chapter 5 of *Sexy Christians*.

Week 6: Understanding, Part A   Meeting Date:

_____

Home Play Assignment: Before this session, read chapter 3, Understanding, from the beginning of the chapter through Personal Touch on page 60.

Recommended Reading: Chapters 6–7 of *Sexy Christians*.

Week 7: Understanding, Part B   Meeting Date:

_____

Home Play Assignment: Before this session, read the rest of chapter 3, Understanding, from page 61 through the end of the chapter.

Recommended Reading: Chapter 8 of *Sexy Christians*.

Week 8: Critical Conversations, Part A   Meeting Date:

Home Play Assignment: Before this session, read chapter 4, Critical Conversations, from the beginning of the chapter through Personal Touch at the top of page 87.

Recommended Reading: Chapters 9–10 of *Sexy Christians*.

Week 9: Critical Conversations, Part B   Meeting Date:

Home Play Assignment: Before this session, read the rest of chapter 4, Critical Conversations, from Touch Up on page 87 through the end of the chapter.

Recommended Reading: Chapter 11 of *Sexy Christians*.

Week 10: Honesty, Part A   Meeting Date:

Home Play Assignment: Before this session, read chapter 5, Honesty, from the beginning of the chapter through Personal Touch on page 107.

Recommended Reading: Chapter 12 of *Sexy Christians*.

Week 11: Honesty, Part B   Meeting Date:

Home Play Assignment: Before this session, read the rest of chapter 5, Honesty, from Touch Up on page 108 through the end of the chapter.

Recommended Reading: Complete any unfinished chapters in *Sexy Christians* over the final weeks of the study.

Week 12: Sexy Christians Celebration   Meeting Date:
_____

> Home Play Assignment: Complete the Personal Touch exercise in appendix 3. Work to catch up on any incomplete Personal Touch exercises.
>
> Recommended Reading: Complete any unfinished chapters in *Sexy Christians* over the final weeks of the study.

Notes

Introduction

1. Marilyn vos Savant, www.thinkexist.com/English/Author/x/Author_3607_1. htm (accessed April 28, 2009).

2. J. A. Mangels, B. Butterfield, J. Lamb, C. Good, and C. S. Dweck, "Why Do Beliefs and Intelligence Influence Learning Success? A Social Cognitive Neuroscience Model," *Social Cognitive and Affective Neuroscience* 1, no. 2:75–86.

3. David Schnarch, *Resurrecting Sex* (New York: Quill, 2003), 15–18. Robert T. Michael, John H. Gagnon, Edward O. Lawmann, and Gina Kilater, *Sex in America: A Definitive Survey* (Boston: Little, Brown and Company, 1995), 39.

4. Ruth Houston, "Infidelity Trends to Watch," www.infidelitytrends.com (accessed January 23, 2009).

5. A. B. Francken, H. B. van de Wiel, and W. C. Weijmar Schultz, "What Importance Do Women Attribute to the Size of the Penis?" *European Urology* 45, no. 5:426–31.

6. Beth A. Morhr, Shalender Bhasen, Carol L. Link, Amy B. O'Donnell, and John B. McKinlay, "The Effects of Changes in Adiposity on Testosterone Levels in Older Men," *European Journal of Endocrinology* 155, no. 3:443–52.

7. Schnarch, *Resurrecting Sex*, 18.

Chapter 1 Trust

1. Louis Cozolino, *The Neuroscience of Human Relationships* (New York: W. W. Norton, 2006), 93–96.

2. Answers to Personal Touch Quiz: Noah, d; Abraham, e; Hosea, c; Nicodemus, a; Peter and Andrew, b.

3. W. F. Arndt and F. W. Gingrich, *A Greek-English Lexicon of the New Testament and Other Early Christian Literature* (Chicago: University of Chicago Press, 1957), 783.

4. Craig S. Keener, *The IVP Bible Background Commentary: New Testament* (Downer's Grove, IL: InterVarsity, 1993), 237.

Chapter 2 Openness

1. Chris Frith, *Making Up the Mind* (Oxford: Blackwell, 2007), 9.

2. Daniel Siegel, *The Developing Mind: Toward a Neurobiology of Interpersonal Experience* (New York: Guilford Press, 1999), 28–66.

3. C. A. Nelson and L. J. Carver, "The Effects of Stress and Trauma on Brain and Memory: A View from Developmental Cognitive Neuroscience," *Development and Psychopathology* 10:793–810.

4. I. G. Russek and G. E. Schwartz, "Feelings of Parental Caring Predict Health Status in Midlife: A 35-year Follow-up of the Harvard Mastery of Stress Study," *Journal of Behavioral Medicine* 20:1–13.

5. Cozolino, *Neuroscience of Human Relationships*, 71.

6. I. Kimura, M. Kubota, H. Hirose, M. Yumoto, and Y. Sakakihara, "Children Are Sensitive to Averted Eyes at the Earliest Stage of Gaze Processing," *NeuroReport* 15:1345–48.

7. Louis Cozolino, "The Tie between Neuroscience and Psychotherapy," IITAP Conference, Phoenix, AZ, February 2008.

8. The language is forceful but not violent. It is a common word, *laquah*, in an uncommon context: the covenant kindness (*hesed*) of God. Bill T. Arnold, *The NIV Application Commentary: 1 & 2 Samuel* (Grand Rapids: Zondervan, 2003), 508.

Chapter 3 Understanding

1. Beverly Hubble Tauke, *Healing Your Family Tree: A Destiny-Changing Journey toward Freedom, Forgiveness, and Healthier Relationships* (Carol Stream, IL: Tyndale House, 2004), 32.

Chapter 4 Critical Conversations

1. Dean Ornish, *Love and Survival: The Healing Power of Intimacy* (New York: HarperCollins, 1998), 63.

2. John Gottman and Nan Silver, *The Seven Principles for Making Marriage Work* (New York: Three Rivers Press, 1999), 11.

3. Ibid., 26–46.

4. Richard Behan, Ben Fong Torres, and Margaret Law, *The Neuropsychology of Self-Discipline* (Newark, CA: SyberVision Systems, 1985).

5. Henri Nouwen, *Spiritual Direction: Wisdom for the Long Walk of Faith* (San Francisco: Harper, 2006), 114.

6. Michael Dye, *The Genesis Process: For Change Groups Book 2 Individual Workbook* (Auburn, CA: Genesis Addiction Process and Programs, 2006), 71.

Chapter 5 Honesty

1. Scott Peck, *Further Along the Road Less Traveled: The Unending Journey toward Spiritual Growth* (New York: Simon and Schuster, 1993), 98–101.

Tell Me More

DR. TED ROBERTS AND
DIANE ROBERTS

How can I become a Sexy Christian?

Along with this workbook, pick up our book *Sexy Christians: The Purpose, Power, and Passion of Biblical Intimacy* (Grand Rapids: Baker, 2010). It's available in bookstores or online wherever Christian books are sold. And make sure to visit www.sexychristians.com, our online home. It's the place to order additional books and other Sexy Christians materials, download video podcasts of our teaching, and become part of the continuing Sexy Christians conversation.

How can I attend a Sexy Christians Seminar?

Check out our speaking schedule online at www.sexy christians.com or www.puredesire.org, the online home of Pure Desire Ministries International (PDMI). If you don't see anything in your area, click "Host a Seminar" and invite us soon.

I'm struggling with a sexual addiction. Where can I go for help?

Go to www.puredesire.org and click on "Find a Pure Desire Group." This page will help you find PDMI affiliates that offer Pure Desire groups for men and women. Click on your state to find local groups. If you need more help, view our online materials or call our ministry office at 1-503-489-0235.

I'm a pastor or other large group leader. How can I host a Sexy Christians Seminar?

Check out the information online at www.sexychristians.com, "Host a Seminar." Fill out the information request and a PDMI staff member will contact you soon. You can also email our staff at kathyw@puredesire.org.

I teach a small group or adult Sunday school class. Where do I go for help?

Appendix 1 of this workbook offers specific tips for small group leaders. Also, the Leader Lines scattered throughout the workbook will help you guide your group smoothly. Check out www.sexychristians.com for further leaders' helps and free downloads. Finally, contact Direct2Church (a division of Baker Publishing Group) for information on orders and special group pricing at www.direct2church.com, or call 1-800-877-2665.

Dr. Ted Roberts likes to say he was "drafted into the pastorate" from his career as a Marine fighter pilot. During his years as senior pastor of East Hill Church in Gresham, Oregon, the church grew to more than 6,000 members. President and cofounder of Pure Desire Ministries International, Ted is a certified Sex Addiction Therapist whose previous books include *Pure Desire*, *Seven Pillars of Freedom*, *For Men Only*, *Living Life Boldly*, *Going Deeper*, and *Failing Forward*. Ted is a sought-after speaker who, with his wife, Diane, travels across the globe to lead Sexy Christians Conferences.

Diane Roberts provides the perfect balance for her husband in both marriage and ministry. Cofounder of Pure Desire Ministries International, she served alongside Ted as women's ministry director, pastor, and counselor at East Hill Church for more than twenty years. She is the author of *Betrayed Heart*, *Betrayal and Beyond: Healing for Broken Trust*, and *Accept No Substitutes* and contributing author of *Pure Desire*. Her humor, insights, and experience combine to make Diane a popular speaker and dynamic coleader of Sexy Christians Conferences. She and Ted have two grown children and four grandchildren.

This workbook can change your life and your marriage. But don't stop here. Buy the book that started it all.

Visit www.puredesire.org for more information.

Available wherever books are sold.

Direct 2 Church
○ Resources for Christian Communities

For case quantity discounts of **30–50% off**
the regular retail price for your church or group,
please visit www.direct2church.com or email us at
Direct2Church@BakerPublishingGroup.com.

DR. TED ROBERTS &
DIANE ROBERTS

SEXY
christians

THE PURPOSE, POWER, and PASSION
of BIBLICAL INTIMACY

BakerBooks
a division of Baker Publishing Group
www.BakerBooks.com

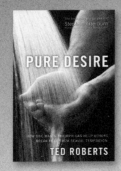